Teddy Cameron Long

Sterling Publishing Co., Inc. New York
A STERLING/TAMOS BOOK

A Sterling/Tamos Book
© 1997 Teddy Cameron Long

Sterling Publishing Co., Inc.
387 Park Avenue South,
New York, NY 10016 8810

TAMOS Books Inc.
300 Wales Avenue, Winnipeg, MB,
Canada R2M 2S9

10 9 8 7 6 5 4 3 2 1

Distributed in Canada by
Sterling Publishing Co., Inc.
c/o Canadian Manda Group
One Atlantic Avenue, Suite 105
Toronto, Ontario, Canada M6K 3E7
Distributed in Great Britain and Europe
by Cassell PLC
Wellington House, 125 Strand,
London WC2R 0BB, England
Distributed in Australia by Capricorn
Link (Australia) Pty Ltd.
P.O. Box 6651, Baulkham Hills,
Business Centre, NSW 2153, Australia

Design A. O. Osen
Illustrations Teddy Cameron Long
Photography Jerry Grajewski,
Custom Images Ltd.
Printed in Hong Kong

Canadian Cataloging-in-Publication Data
Long, Teddy Cameron
    Super masks and fun face painting
    "A Sterling/Tamos book."
    Includes index.
        ISBN 1-895569-09-5
1. Mask making. 2. Face painting. I. Title.
TT898.L65 1997   745.59 C96-920007-2

Library of Congress Cataloging-in-
Publication Data
Long, Teddy Cameron.
    Super masks and fun face painting /
Teddy Cameron Long.
        p.   cm.
    "A Sterling/Tamos book."
    Includes index.
        ISBN 1-895569-09-5
    1. Mask making. 2. Masks.
3. Face painting. I. Title.
TT898.L65   1997
646.4'78--DC20   96-35803
                                CIP

ISBN 1-895569-09-5

Contents

Introduction

Since prehistoric times, masks have been an important part of different cultures of the world, often playing a vital role in people's daily lives. Masks were extraordinary symbols of position, importance, influence, and power. Depending on the time and place, they were created to frighten, cajole, entreat, or amuse. Some were a serious part of rituals that influenced decisions and events. Others helped create fantasies for amusement. Still others made disguises for fun and mischief. Whether they were crafted from found materials or painted directly on the face, the object was, and still is, to conceal the wearer's real identity and help create the illusion of being someone or something else with different powers and attributes. This was part of the mystique of shamen, tribal medicine men, and chieftain priests who performed daunting deeds and sacred rites through the persona created by the mask. Many believed that the person wearing the mask became the spirit that the mask invoked, that magical powers were transferred, and that masks were powerful medicine. Often only certain members of a society could make and wear them so that the magic would not fall into the wrong hands. This made the wearer even more significant. He was often held in awe and the masks were treated as sacred icons, brought out and used in ritualistic behavior at important ceremonies and events. They were part of religious worship, marriage, death, birth, coming of age, illness, harvest, spring solstice, and other occasions. There were masks for the dead to help them through the afterlife and animal masks for hunters to allow them to take on the attributes of the animal and give them equal abilities with the beasts they hunted.

In ancient plays, masks portraying a particular emotion helped define the villain or the hero. Actual physical characterization was therefore not necessary. In fact, with the aid of masks one actor could play more than one role. When the Greeks built their amphitheaters, megaphones were built into the actors' masks so they could be heard in the farthest seats.

Today masks and face painting are used mainly for fun. This is often connected with celebrations such as carnivals, parades, and Mardi Gras celebrations where people dress in elaborate costumes and disguise their faces to denote some past event. But there is also a serious side. Masks are used in some sports and as protection on some jobs. These masks are often artfully decorated but usually serve no other purpose than protection.

The art of making masks remains popular. Many materials are used including cardboard, papier mâché, cloth, even wood. The masks in this book demonstrate various simple techniques and represent different cultures and different events. Follow the basic instructions to represent a culture or character for a play, a puppet show, a party, or a holiday. It's great fun and they are all easy to make.

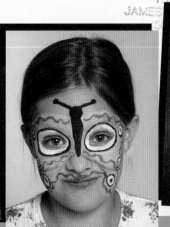

Mask Proportions

When designing a mask it is essential that the mask fit well and allow good vision for the wearer. Before beginning a mask for a particular person, take a few measurements of the person's head and note the distance between the eyes, nose, and mouth.

The diagram at right gives an example of a head with the measurements you should take before designing your mask.

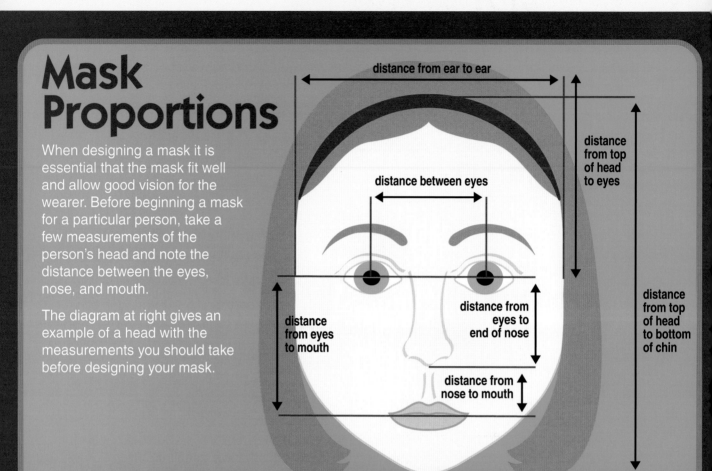

distance from ear to ear

distance between eyes

distance from top of head to eyes

distance from eyes to mouth

distance from eyes to end of nose

distance from top of head to bottom of chin

distance from nose to mouth

Materials and Tools

Materials and tools needed for each project are listed at the beginning of the project. Be sure to have the materials at hand before beginning the project. Materials for the projects in this book are inexpensive and easy to find at craft, hardware, or department stores, or around your house.

Paint—Projects in this book were painted using acrylic art paint. Powdered tempera paint can also be used. If you use powdered tempera, coat the project with white shellac after painting. Clean brushes with methyl hydrate after using shellac.

Primer—You may need to coat the project with a white acrylic primer before painting. This primer can be white latex house paint.

Making a Basic Paper Strip Mask

MATERIALS
bond paper or a roll of shelf paper • ruler • pencil
• scissors • glue stick • paper hole punch
• 12 in (30 cm) elastic cord

1 Cut a strip of paper long enough to wrap around the head from top to bottom and overlap 1 in (2.5 cm). Wrap the strip around the head, as shown. Overlap the ends and glue together with the glue stick.

2 Cut another strip of paper long enough to wrap around the head at the forehead and overlap 1 in (2.5 cm). Glue one end of the second strip to the first strip, as shown, wrapping the strip around the head at the forehead.

3 Glue the second strip to the first strip where they cross, and overlap the ends of the second strip and glue, as shown.

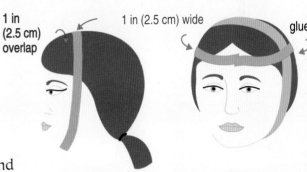

1 in (2.5 cm) overlap

1 in (2.5 cm) wide

glue

4 Cut another strip of paper and glue one end of the strip to the center of the forehead strip. Lay the strip down along the nose and under the chin. Glue the other end of the strip to the paper strip under the chin.

5 Cut more strips of paper and wrap one strip across the face below the nose and glue the ends to the strips along the side of the head.

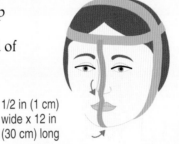

1/2 in (1 cm) wide x 12 in (30 cm) long

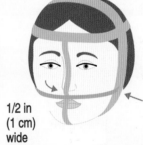

1/2 in (1 cm) wide

6 Place more strips of paper across the face and glue them to the strips already in place. Make a network of strips covering most of the face. Do not cover eyes or mouth.

7 Fill in small holes in the paper mask with torn pieces of paper glued in place using the glue stick.

8 To remove the mask, cut or tear the strip of paper at the back of the head, and carefully pull the mask off the face.

9 Trim the eyes and mouth openings with scissors after the mask has been removed from the face. Cut off the hanging strips and trim the edges.

10 Using a paper hole punch, make a small hole on each side of the mask at the same level as the eyes. Tie a piece of elastic cord to one of the holes in the side. Fit the mask to the head, adjust the length of elastic. Cut off excess elastic, and tie the other end of the elastic to the other hole.

11 The mask is ready to be decorated.

Making a Basic Paper Sheet Mask

MATERIALS
8-1/2 x 11 in (21.5 x 30 cm) sheet of bond paper or stiff paper or flexible poster board • ruler • pencil • scissors • paper hole punch • craft glue • masking tape • 12 in (30 cm) elastic cord

1 Draw a line down the center of the sheet of paper or poster board. Draw a second line across the center of the sheet, as shown. The nose is placed at the horizontal line.

2 Draw eyes above the nose line, as shown. Draw the mouth below the nose line, as shown.

3 Draw a triangle from each side of the mask to the nose, as shown.

4 Draw a chin along the bottom of the sheet.

5 Cut out the eyes, mouth, triangles, and chin. With a paper hole punch, make a hole on each side of the mask at the same level as the eyes.

6 Overlap the edges of the triangles and glue in place. Hold the glued edges together with tape until the glue is dry. Remove tape.

7 Tie a piece of elastic cord to one of the holes on the side.

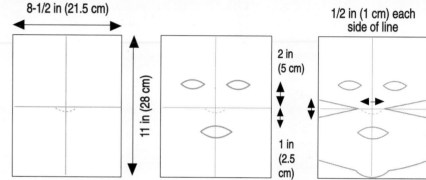

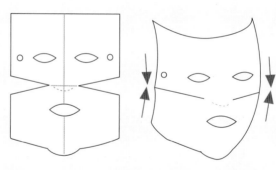

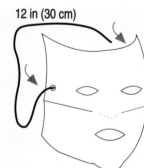

8 Fit the mask to the head, adjust the length of elastic. Cut off excess elastic and tie the other end of the elastic to the other hole.

9 The mask is ready to be decorated.

Making Papier-Mâché Masks

MATERIALS FOR MAKING THE PULP
newspaper • ruler • water • 1 gallon (4 l) pail • measuring cups • box of wallpaper paste • plastic wrap

PULP METHOD
Preparing the pulp

1 Tear up old newspaper into pieces. Fill the pail about half full. This will make enough pulp to make one average mask.

2 Add enough water to cover the pulp and let stand several hours or overnight. When the paper is soft and wet, crush and mix the paper and water together to make a soft mixture like porridge. When the paper is broken up into fragments, drain off most of the water through an old sieve.

3 Add powdered wallpaper paste to bind the paper pulp together. Add about 1/4 cup of powder to 1 cup of pulp. Knead the mixture together until it is like clay. Add more wallpaper paste or more water as required to adjust the texture of the pulp.

4 Cover pulp with plastic wrap to prevent drying. Pulp will keep at room temperature two days, or stored in a refrigerator or freezer until needed.

5 Papier-mâché pulp may take several days to dry. The length of time required depends on the thickness of the pulp, the amount of water in the mixture, and the humidity. Once it is dry, it is extremely hard and durable, and can be sanded smooth before painting.

Making a Basic Papier-Mâché Pulp Mask

> **MATERIALS FOR PULP METHOD**
> newspaper • tape • plastic wrap • papier-mâché pulp • plasticine • pencil • 12 in (30 cm) elastic cord • scissors

1 Papier-mâché pulp must be molded over a structure of some kind. Crumple several sheets of newspaper tightly together and tape into a large ball. Cover the newspaper ball with plastic wrap.

2 Working on a plastic-covered work surface, model the papier-mâché pulp over the plastic. This will create a very flat mask.

3 More definition can be created using plasticine. Model a layer of plasticine over the plastic-covered newspaper ball forming a nose, lips, and eyebrows, or other desired features.

4 Cover the plasticine directly with the papier-mâché pulp. While pulp is still wet, use the end of a pencil to punch a small hole on each side of the mask at the same level as the eyes.

5 When pulp is dry, the plasticine can be peeled off the back of the mask. Tie a piece of elastic cord to one of the holes in the side. Fit the mask to the head, adjust the length of elastic. Cut off excess elastic, and tie the other end of the elastic to the other hole.

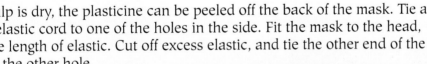

OPTIONAL MODELING FORM
An easy way to mold a mask is to use a styrofoam head form, available from wig shops or craft suppliers. This is a good short-cut if you have several masks to make. The styrofoam can be covered with plasticine to make the desired alterations and features. Remember to measure the styrofoam head to check if it is actually life-size. You may have to enlarge the face with a layer of plasticine.

Making a Basic Papier-Mâché Strip Mask

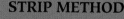

MATERIALS FOR STRIP METHOD
balloon or styrofoam head form or plastic-covered ball of newspaper (p7) • newspaper • 1 gallon (4 *l*) pail • measuring cups • box of wallpaper paste • water • plastic wrap • plasticine • fine sandpaper • pencil • 12 in (30 cm) elastic cord • scissors

STRIP METHOD

Papier-mâché strip method takes less preparation than papier-mâché pulp method. The form is prepared in the same way. You may wish to spend a little more time on the detail of the plasticine mold since it is harder to make details with strips than with pulp.

1 Select the head form and place on a plastic-covered work surface.

2 Tear newspapers into strips. For sections with tight corners or detail such as the nose area, tear the paper into narrower strips.

3 Mix the wallpaper paste according to package directions. Dip newspaper strips into the wallpaper paste and pull the strips between two fingers to remove excess paste, as shown.

4 Lay strips across the form overlapping each other. Cover the form with at least 6 layers of newspaper strips.

5 While strips are still wet, use the end of a pencil to punch a small hole on each side of the mask at the same level as the eyes. Set aside in a warm dry place to harden. Like papier-mâché pulp, newspaper strips can take several days to dry, depending on thickness, moisture content, and humidity.

6 When dry, remove the mask from the plasticine form. If a smooth surface is desired, sand the mask. Attach other items, if required.

7 Tie a piece of elastic cord to one of the holes in the side of the dry mask. Fit the mask to the head, adjust the length of elastic. Cut off excess elastic, and tie the other end of the elastic to the other hole.

8 The mask is ready to be decorated.

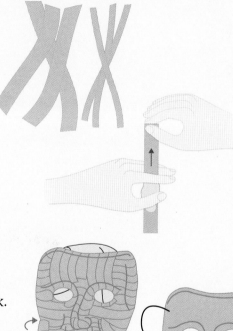

STRIP METHOD OVER A BALLOON

1 Blow up the balloon and knot the end. This is the head form structure. Set the balloon on a plastic-covered work surface and cover the balloon with strips of newspaper dipped in wallpaper paste. Leave the balloon knot uncovered.

2 When there are at least 6 layers of paper covering the balloon, tie a string to the knotted end of the balloon and hang to dry. When the papier-mâché is hard, cut off the knot from the balloon.

3 With a sharp knife *carefully* cut a small opening in the open end of the shell. Remove the balloon from the inside of the paper shell. Proceed with the desired mask project.

Making a Basic Paper Plate Mask

MATERIALS
1—10 in (25.5 cm) paper plate • ruler • pencil • scissors • sheet of heavy paper • paper hole punch • craft glue • masking tape • 12 in (30 cm) elastic cord

1 Turn the paper plate bottom side up. In the center of the plate, draw a face to fit the wearer, as described on p4, (Mask Proportions).

2 Draw the nose to fit the full length of the wearer's nose, as shown. Cut out eyes, nose, and mouth.

3 Cut out a triangle from the heavy paper that is twice the width of the nose and 1/2 in (1 cm) longer.

4 Glue the edge of the paper around the top and sides of the nose opening, making an arch.

5 With a paper hole punch, make a hole on each side of the mask at the same level as the eyes. Tie a piece of elastic cord to one of the holes at the side. Fit the mask to the head, adjust the length of elastic. Cut off excess elastic, and tie the other end of the elastic to the other hole.

6 The mask is ready to be decorated.

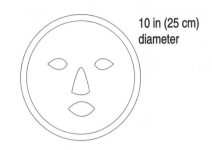

10 in (25 cm) diameter

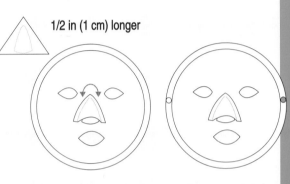

1/2 in (1 cm) longer

Making a Basic Thai Theater Mask

MATERIALS
26 in (66 cm) x 22 in (56 in) flexible light poster board • ruler • pencil • scissors • craft glue • masking tape • newspaper • box of wallpaper paste • water • 1 gallon (4 *l*) pail

This mask is based on masks used in classical dance theater in Thailand.

1 Using the sheet of poster board, measure and mark a line down one long side, dividing the sheet into two pieces, as shown.

2 Draw lines across the smaller section to create tabs, as shown. Cut along the sides of the tabs to make a total of 13 tabs.

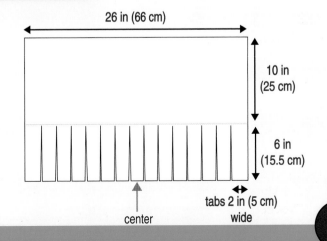

26 in (66 cm)

10 in (25 cm)

6 in (15.5 cm)

tabs 2 in (5 cm) wide

center

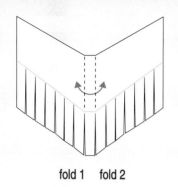
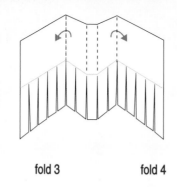

fold 1   fold 2   fold 3   fold 4

3 Find the center tab and fold the sheet backwards along both sides of this tab (folds 1 and 2), as shown.

4 Make a third fold across the sheet forward along the side of another tab 4 in (10 cm) away from fold 1, as shown.

5 Make a fourth fold across the sheet forward along the side of another tab 4 in (10 cm) away from fold 2, as shown.

1 in (2.5 cm) overlap

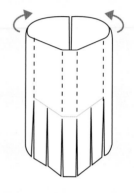

6 Bring the short ends of the sheet together and overlap 1 in (2.5 cm), making a cylinder. Glue the ends together and hold with tape until the glue dries.

7 Place the cylinder with the tabs facing up. Bend the tabs over towards the center, making a gentle curved top. Glue and tape the ends to one another to hold in place.

8 Place the mask over the head to mark the position of the eyes and mouth. See p4 (Proportions). Remove the mask. Draw the eyes as circles and the mouth shape, as shown.

9 Cut out the eye holes and cut along the solid lines of the mouth where indicated.

10 Bend the tabs of the mouth inward using the dotted lines as a guide, and tape in place.

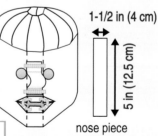

cut along solid lines, fold along dotted lines

11 Using a piece of poster board, make the nose, as shown. Tape the top of this piece between the eyes. Bend into a curve and tape the other end of the piece above the mouth, as shown. Cover sides of nose with more tape.

12 Using the pattern as a guide, draw and cut out 2 ears from poster board. Fold the ears along the line indicated, and tape to the side of the head, as shown.

13 Tear up newspaper into strips 1 in (2.5 cm) wide. Mix the wallpaper paste according to package directions.

1-1/2 in (4 cm)

5 in (12.5 cm)

nose piece

14 On a plastic-covered work surface, cover the mask head with strips of newspaper dipped in wallpaper paste (see Basic Papier-mâché Strip Mask, p7). The mask is ready for decorating.

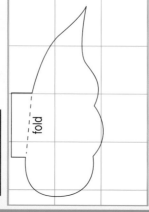

EAR PATTERN
each square equals
1 inch (2.5 cm)

fold

Face Painting Basics

The face painting designs in this book were done using water-based paints specially designed for use on the skin. You may have make-up at home that can be used for face painting, such as lipstick and eye shadow. Eyeliner pencils can be very useful for drawing and outlining a design. There are also water-soluable crayons and sets of paints that look like a box of watercolor paints available for face painting. These come in many bright colors, and are easy to use.

Before applying a new substance to the face, it is always wise to check for an allergic reaction. Apply a small amount of paint to the wrist, wait an hour, and then wash the paint off. Check this area for irritation before using the paint on your face. Follow any manufacturer's instructions.

How to prepare for Face Painting

MATERIALS
water-based face paints • water • 2 or 3 soft brushes—1 flat, 1 round • make-up sponges • facial tissues • a head band or scarf to keep hair back • cotton swabs

1 Set up two chairs facing each other and close together. Choose a chair with arms for the person applying the face paint. Have a low table next to the chairs on which to place the materials. Set the person to be painted comfortably in the chair across from you, resting their hands on their knees or elbows on the arms of their chair. Face painting takes time. It is important that both people are comfortable.

2 Secure the hair back from the face, using a head band or scarf.

3 Dip the crayon or brush in water and begin. Follow the instructions to create the design. (Make-up sponges work well to color large areas. Wet the sponge in water, squeeze out any excess, and rub the sponge against the paint. Apply to the face.)

4 Use cotton swabs dipped in water to correct any mistakes.

5 To remove the face paint, wash the face with soap and water.

Ancient Ceremonies

In cultures such as the indigenous people of the northwest coast of North America, masks were used to pass cultural information down through the generations. Legends, myths, and family history were documented through masks. The images could be creatures in the natural world such as animals and birds, elements of nature such as the sun or storms, or they could represent spirits. Masks made the spirit world visible and gave it life.

In some cultures, masks were used only by shaman. Some masks depicted the transformation of a creature into another form. These masks have sections that opened up to reveal another mask inside the first one. The masks gave the wearer special powers. Mask wearing was often accompanied by song and dance.

MASK

This mask is based on the traditional mask forms of the Haida people. It is not a copy of any Haida mask, which is individual to a family's history.

TECHNIQUE Cut pattern mask

MATERIALS 28 x 22 in (71 x 56 cm) sheet of flexible poster board • ruler • pencil • scissors • table knife • craft glue • masking tape • paint

1 Using the pattern on page 14, enlarge the design on a sheet of grid paper, or use a photocopier machine.

2 Fold the sheet of poster board in half. Draw the pattern along the fold line, as shown.

3 Cut out the pattern, cutting through both layers of the poster board. Do not cut through the fold lines around the mouth.

4 Unfold the sheet and draw the pattern on the other side of the sheet. Cut out the eye holes.

5 To make a curved crease, gently score along the fold line with a table knife. Do not cut through the poster board. Run your thumbnail along the fold line of the poster board bending the other side up against your thumb, as shown.

6 Paint the flat mask.

7 Overlap the the flaps along the top edge of the mask, as shown. Glue in place.

8 Cut out a half oval 4 in (10 cm) and 2 in (5 cm) wide. Glue to the inside of the mouth.

9 Attach the elastic cord, *see p6.*

13

HAIDA MASK PATTERN
each square equals
1 inch (2.5 cm)

FACE PAINTING

TECHNIQUE Whole face painting

MATERIALS water-based face paints:
white, black, blue, red • make-up
sponge • paint brushes • headband •
tissues • cotton swabs

1 See p11 for basic face painting techniques.

2 Using the make-up sponge, paint the face white.

3 Using black paint, draw heavy black eyebrows. Draw a double-arched shape under the eyes. Draw a curved T-shape between the eyes. Fill in the shapes with solid black.

4 Using red, paint a curved U-shape on the forehead, as shown. Draw a large red mouth, and fill in with solid red. Using black, draw black semi-circles around the red mouth shape.

5 Using blue paint, outline the eyes. Paint curved blue shapes on each side of the nose.

NAVAJO

MASK

The design of this mask is influenced by the art developed by the Navajo people. It is not a copy of masks made and used by medicine men.

TECHNIQUE Sewn

MATERIALS felt 28 in x 12 in (71cm x 30cm) • ruler • marking pencil • scissors • needle • pins • thread • darning needle • embroidery yarn • fake fur • feathers

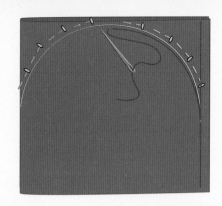
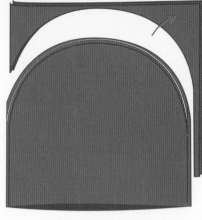

1. Fold the felt in half, short ends together and pin. Sew the two ends together.

2. Using the marking pencil, draw an arc across the top of the felt, as shown. Pin around the outside of the mark. Sew around the top, following the drawn arc.

3. Remove the pins. Cut around the outside of the sewn arc, making a hood.

4. Turn the hood right side out. Place over the head and mark the position of the eyes and mouth using the marking pencil. Remove the hood.

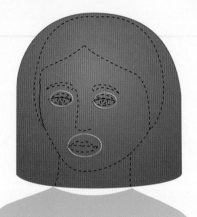
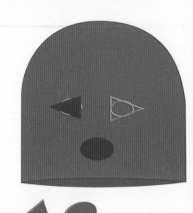

5. Draw 2 triangles for eyes and a circle for the mouth. Cut out the shapes.

6. Using the darning needle and embroidery yarn, sew around the eye and mouth openings using a blanket stitch, as shown.

7. With more embroidery yarn, sew a rectangle between the eyes, and sew horizontal lines connecting the sides of the vertical lines, as shown.

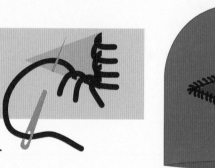

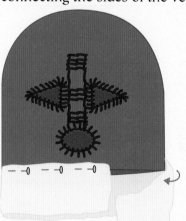
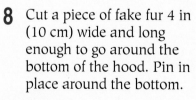

8. Cut a piece of fake fur 4 in (10 cm) wide and long enough to go around the bottom of the hood. Pin in place around the bottom.

9. Sew the strip of fur to the bottom of the hood.

10. Sew the feathers to one side of the mask, as shown.

Masks for the Dead

Masks for the dead have been used all over the world, from Africa to the islands of the South Pacific. They were thought to provide a link with the spirit world or the afterlife, and help the spirit of a dead person make the journey from this life to the next. Masks also served as protection for the dead person and were used to frighten away evil spirits that might do harm.

In some cultures masks were used to call up the spirits of dead ancestors. These masks were often elaborate—carved in wood or made of wicker, some 20 feet high. They were often decorated with shells, feathers, and precious metals.

KING TUT

MASK & COLLAR

This mask is based on the funeral mask of King Tutankhamen, who died in Egypt in the 14th century BC. His tomb contained many likenesses of the king. The funeral masks were made of wood, alabaster, and gold, and decorated with semi-precious stones and colored glass.

TECHNIQUE Basic paper strip mask

MATERIALS 8-1/2 x 11 in (21.5 x 30 cm) sheets of bond paper or stiff paper • glue stick • 28 x 22 in (71 x 56 cm) flexible light poster board • table knife • paper towel cardboard tube • ruler • pencil • scissors • paper hole punch • craft glue • craft knife • tape • 12 in (30 cm) elastic cord • blue, turquoise paint • metallic gold paint

1 Make a basic paper strip mask, p5.

2 Transfer the pattern (p20) for the headdress to the sheet of poster board. Cut out. Make the folds and cuts where indicated on the pattern.

3 To make a curved crease, gently score along the fold line with a table knife. Do not cut through the poster board. Run your thumbnail along the fold line of the poster board bending the other side up against your thumb, as shown.

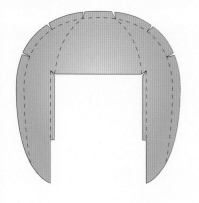
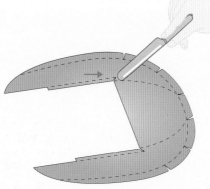
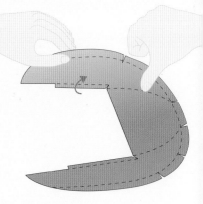

4 Spread glue on the forehead of the paper mask. Bend the front of the poster board headdress over the mask face and press in place. Hold in position with tape.

5 Fold the tabs along the inside of the headdress and glue in place along the sides of the mask face.

6 Fold the top edge of the headdress back. Overlap the edges of the cuts, as shown. Glue and tape.

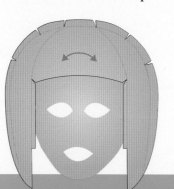
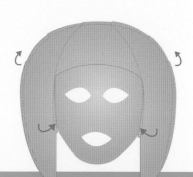

7 Using the cardboard tube, measure and cut the tube, as shown, to make the beard. Make a cut at one end, as shown.

8 Overlap the cut edges and glue and tape to make the tube tapered, as shown.

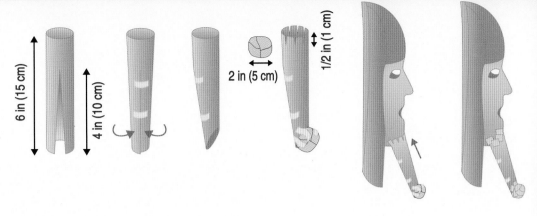

6 in (15 cm)

4 in (10 cm)

2 in (5 cm)

1/2 in (1 cm)

9 Cut off the narrow end of the cylinder at an angle, as shown.

10 Crumple a piece of newspaper into a ball and place the paper ball in the narrow end of the tube, as shown, and tape in place.

11 Make cuts around the wide end of the tube, as shown.

12 Spread glue around the inside of the tabs on the wide end. Place the end of the tube against the chin of the paper mask and press the tabs in place, as shown. Tape in place until the glue dries.

13 Cover the joins where the tube meets the face and the paper ball meets the end of the tube with small pieces of paper spread with craft glue.

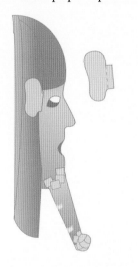

14 Transfer the pattern (p21) for the ears onto scraps of poster board. Cut out. Bend the tabs on the ears back and glue to the side of the head, as shown.

15 Transfer the patterns (p21) for the snake and vulture onto scraps of poster board. There are two pattern pieces for each animal.

16 Cut out the pieces. Using a craft knife, *carefully* make the slits in the back piece where indicated.

17 Bend the back piece over the back edge of the front piece, sliding the tabs on the front piece through the slots on the back piece.

18 Bend the tabs on the front piece over and glue to the back side of the back piece, as shown. Tape the tabs to hold in place until the glue dries. The snake and the vulture are constructed in the same way.

19 Glue them to the front of the headdress. The vulture is placed over the right eye and the snake over the left eye.

20 If the neck piece is desired, transfer the pattern (p21) onto a piece of poster board and cut out.

21 Paint the mask and neck piece. The mask is painted gold with blue lines around the eyes and eyebrows. Headdress is gold with turquoise stripes. Color for the the neck piece, snake, and vulture is shown on the patterns.

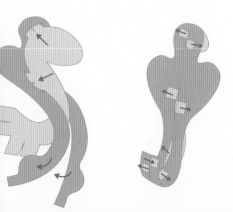

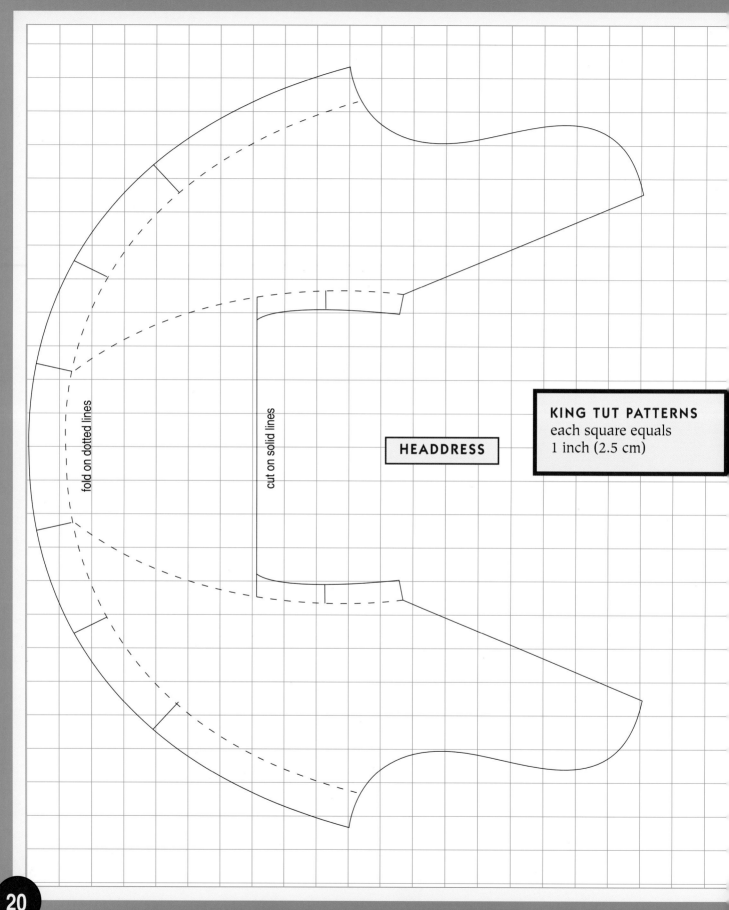

fold on dotted lines

cut on solid lines

HEADDRESS

KING TUT PATTERNS
each square equals
1 inch (2.5 cm)

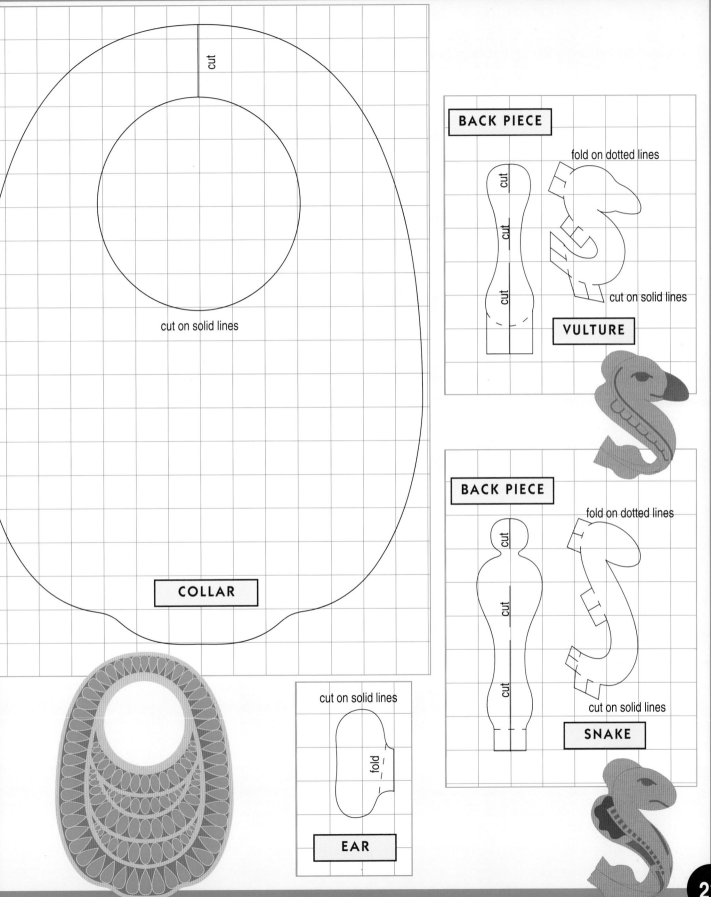

cut

cut on solid lines

COLLAR

BACK PIECE

fold on dotted lines

cut

cut

cut

cut on solid lines

VULTURE

BACK PIECE

fold on dotted lines

cut

cut

cut

cut on solid lines

SNAKE

cut on solid lines

fold

EAR

INCA

MASK

Inca peoples molded masks for the dead from precious metals such as gold, copper, or silver, or carved them from onyx or turquoise. The masks were placed over the faces of the dead.

TECHNIQUE Basic papier-mâché strip mask

MATERIALS plasticine • newspaper • work surface or cutting board • ruler • 1 gallon (4 l) pail • measuring cups • box of wallpaper paste • water • plastic wrap • table knife • scissors • paint • metallic gold paint

1 Cover the cutting board with plastic wrap. Cover the plastic surface with a layer of plasticine 1/4 in (.5 cm) thick, in a square 12 in (30 cm) wide.

2 Model a face in the center of the square. Make geometric shapes around the face, as shown.

3 Cover the plasticine with strips of newspaper dipped in wallpaper paste. While the paper is still wet, press the paper against the plasticene ridges with the edge of the knife.

4 Set aside to dry. When hard, remove the mask from the plasticine form. Trim the edges.

5 Paint to resemble a metal sheet.

12 in (30 cm)

12 in (30 cm)

1/4 in (.5 cm)

Theater Masks

Masks and face painting have been used in theater productions since ancient times. In Greece, where huge amphitheaters could seat thousands of spectators, masks identified the characters so that even people in the farthest seat could follow the storyline that the character represented. There were two main types of plays in Greek theater—comedies and tragedies. These types were represented by stylized masks and such representative masks are sometimes used in theater today.

Masks were also used in medieval Europe to tell bible stories at a time when few people could read and write. Miracle or mystery plays were very popular during the 13th–16th centuries. They enacted stories of the miracles of the saints, or messages from the Old and New Testaments. They were performed outdoors in a sequence of short scenes on festival days or on a wagon or float that could be moved from one place to another. In later years morality plays, that featured the struggle between good and evil, became popular. In the 16th century some Shakespearean plays, such as *A Midsummer Night's Dream* and *Much Ado About Nothing* used masks.

In other cultures, masks are used in traditional theater. In India, in a special form of masked dance drama called Chhau (meaning mask) the performers wear elaborate masks made of modeled clay with layers of gauze and paper to represent the characters. The techniques of mask making are passed down through generations of craftsmen.

Other forms of Indian theater use traditional face-painting mask styles. Each character has a specific design of face painting that can take hours to apply. The face painting is done by several make-up men while the actor lies on his back. Since all roles are played by men, masks and make-up help to create the illusion of female characters.

Thailand has a type of masked pantomime called *Khon*. It evolved from shadow puppet plays of Southeast Asia. In the Thai masked play, dancers, chorus, soloists, and orchestra are all coordinated.

COMEDY·TRAGEDY

MASKS

TECHNIQUE Basic papier-mâché strip mask

MATERIALS plastic-covered ball of newspaper (p7) • newspaper • 1 gallon (4 *l*) pail • measuring cups • box of wallpaper paste • water • plastic wrap • plasticine • 12 in (30 cm) elastic cord (or ribbon) • scissors • pencil • paint

1 Make two basic papier-mâché strip masks, p8.

2 Model each form so that it is longer than the usual proportions. For the comedy mask, model the mouth with upturned corners, raised eyebrows, and facial wrinkles that copy the shapes of the mouth and eyes. For the tragedy mask, model the mouth with downturned corners, wrinkled eyebrows, and facial wrinkles that copy the shapes of the mouth and eyes.

3 Cover the forms with strips of newspaper dipped in wallpaper paste. Set aside to dry.

4 Remove the mask from the form. Trim the edges. Make holes in the mask at the level of the eyes to attach the elastic cord, or ribbon.

5 Prime and paint the mask(s), as desired.

6 Attach the elastic cord or ribbon, p8.

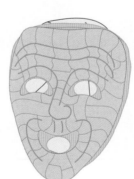
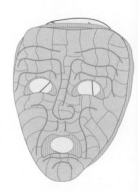

SUN

MASK

TECHNIQUE Basic papier-mâché strip mask

MATERIALS plastic-wrapped styrofoam head form or plastic-covered ball of newspaper (p7) • newspaper • ruler • 1 gallon (4 *l*) pail • measuring cups • box of wallpaper paste • water • plastic wrap • plasticine • fine sandpaper • 12 in (30 cm) elastic cord • scissors • pencil • paper • glue stick • corrugated cardboard • masking tape • paint

1 Make a basic papier-mâché strip mask, p8. Before covering the basic head mask with strips of newspaper and wallpaper paste, make the rays of the sun.

2 Cut a piece of paper long enough to wrap around the styrofoam head form. Wrap this strip around the head from the top to the chin, and back up to the top of the head, as shown. Glue and tape in place.

3 Draw 9 ray shapes on the corrugated cardboard, as shown. Cut out.

4 Glue and tape the bottom edge of each ray to the paper strip so that they point away from the head, as shown.

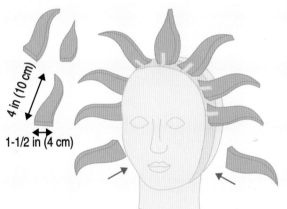

4 in (10 cm)

1-1/2 in (4 cm)

5 Cover the mask face and cardboard rays with strips of newspaper dipped in wallpaper paste, p8. Make the face at least 6 layers thick. Make sure the rays are well attached to the face.

6 Set aside in a warm dry place to harden. Papier-mâché may take several days to dry, depending on thickness, moisture content, and humidity.

7 When the papier-mâché is hard, remove the mask from the head form. If a smooth surface is desired, sand the surface.

8 It is best to make the side holes for the elastic cord once the rays have been attached. See p8 for instructions.

9 Paint and decorate.

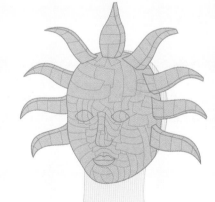

MOON

MASK

1 Make a basic papier-mâché strip mask, p8. Set aside in a warm place to dry.

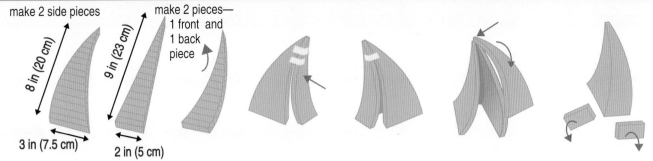

make 2 side pieces

8 in (20 cm)

9 in (23 cm)

make 2 pieces—
1 front and
1 back
piece

3 in (7.5 cm)

2 in (5 cm)

2 To make moon peaks, use corrugated cardboard. Draw the curved sides of the top peak *across* the grain of the cardboard, as shown.

3 Draw the front and back of the top peak *across* the grain of the cardboard, as shown.

4 Gently bend the front and back pieces so that they will wrap along the curve of the sides.

5 Starting at the peak, glue and tape the front section to the edge of the side piece, as shown.

6 Glue and tape the other side piece to the edge of the front section, as shown.

7 Attach the back piece to the edges of the side pieces in the same way.

8 Trim the ends of the front and back sections to fit the side sections.

9 Glue and tape the top peak to the top of the papier-mâché mask.

10 Make the bottom peak in the same way. Remember to draw the curved sides of the bottom peak *across* the grain of the cardboard, as shown.

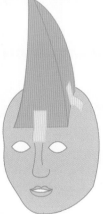

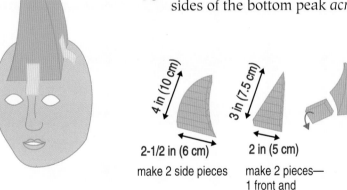

4 in (10 cm)

3 in (7.5 cm)

2-1/2 in (6 cm)

make 2 side pieces

2 in (5 cm)

make 2 pieces—
1 front and
1 back piece

11 Trim the ends of the front section to fit the side sections. *Note* The back section will be shorter than the sides, to allow room for the chin.

12 Glue and tape the bottom peak to the chin of the papier-mâché mask, as shown.

13 Cover both peaks with newspaper strips dipped in wallpaper paste. The cardboard sections need only 2 or 3 layers of paper, but make sure that the cardboard is well covered where it joins the mask.

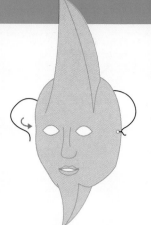

14 Set aside in a warm dry place to harden. Papier mâché may take several days to dry, depending on thickness, moisture content, and humidity.

15 When dry, the mask may be removed from the head form. If a smooth surface is desired, sand the mask. Make side holes for the elastic cord, see p8 for instructions.

16 Paint and decorate.

ANGEL

MASK

Some of the characters in mystery and miracle plays wear masks. This is an example of an angel. Nativity scenes are still performed at Christmas and are represented by traditional characters.

TECHNIQUE Basic papier-mâché strip mask

MATERIALS plastic-wrapped styrofoam head form or plastic-covered ball of newspaper (p7) • newspaper • ruler • 1 gallon (4 *l*) pail • measuring cups • box of wallpaper paste • water • plastic wrap • plasticine • fine sandpaper • pencil • paper • glue stick • corrugated cardboard • masking tape • artificial hair (available in long strands at craft supply stores) • coat hanger • wire cutters • gold ribbon • 12 in (30 cm) elastic cord • scissors • paint

1 Make a basic papier-mâché strip mask, p8.

2 Traditionally, angels have very regular facial characteristics without any large or bony features. For a dramatic look, the brow for this mask has been made somewhat geometric and the nose is straight.

3 Glue the artificial hair to the top of the mask and trim, as shown.

4 Cut a piece of coat hanger 16 in (40 cm) with wire cutters. Bend in an arc. Wrap the wire with gold ribbon. Tape in place. Tape the ends of the halo to the back of the mask.

5 Paint and decorate. Make small side holes to attach the elastic cord, see p8 for instructions.

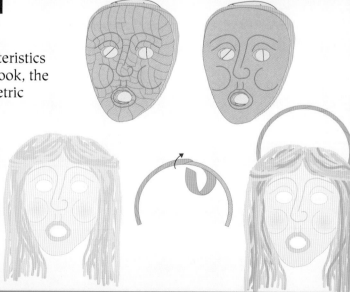

WISE MAN

MASK

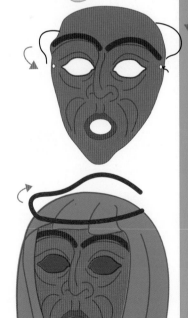

1 Make a basic papier-mâché strip mask, p8. Model the plasticine form with very strong features. Make the top of the head extend far enough back from the eyes to attach a head covering.

2 When the mask is dry, remove from the form. Paint. Add the elastic cord, p7.

3 Place the mask over the face. Drape the fabric over the top of the mask so that the back of the head is covered. Glue in place.

4 Wrap cord around the forehead. Glue in place. Cut off any excess.

MEDUSA

MASK

This mask is based on a character from Greek mythology. Medusa, the most famous of the monster figures known as Gorgons, had snakes for hair. After she was killed anyone who looked at her severed head was turned to stone.

TECHNIQUE Basic papier-mâché pulp mask

MATERIALS plastic-wrapped styrofoam head form or plastic-covered ball of newspaper (p7) • newspaper • ruler • 1 gallon (4 *l*) pail • measuring cups • box of wallpaper paste • water • plastic wrap • plasticine • fine sandpaper • 12 in (30 cm) elastic cord • scissors • pencil • paper • glue stick • corrugated cardboard • masking tape • artificial hair • paint

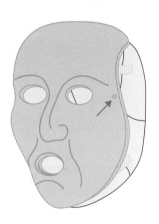

1. Working on a plastic-covered work surface, make a basic papier-mâché pulp mask, p7. This mask covers the top of the head as well as the face. Do not model the head form so that it extends over the back of the head or under the chin, or it will be very difficult to remove the mask from the form.

2. Make a small hole in the papier–mâché pulp on each side of the mask at the same level as the eyes, as shown.

3. On a clean area of the plastic-covered work surface, model snake shapes from extra pulp. Prop some of the heads up with a small ball of plasticine so that some of the snakes are "sitting up." Make a total of 8 snakes.

4. Set aside the head and the snakes to dry.

5. When the pulp is dry, arrange the snakes on the top of the head. Glue in place with craft glue.

6. If desired, glue artificial hair around the snakes.

7. Paint and decorate the head, snakes, and hair. Attach the elastic cord, see p7.

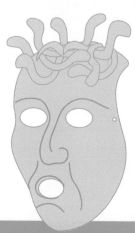

CHHAU

MASK

These stylized, expressionless masks are used in India. They have mostly human features modified to suggest what is being portrayed—a god, hunter, bird, animal, flower. The masks are painted in simple flat colors. Emotions are revealed through gestures and body movement.

TECHNIQUE Basic papier-mâché strip mask

MATERIALS plastic-covered styrofoam head form or plastic-covered ball of newspaper (p7) • newspaper • ruler • 1 gallon (4 *l*) pail • measuring cups • box of wallpaper paste • water • plastic wrap • plasticine • 12 in (30 cm) elastic cord • scissors • corrugated cardboard • pencil • masking tape • paint

1 Make a basic papier-mâché strip mask, p8.

2 Draw the headpiece patterns (p32) on corrugated cardboard. Cut out.

3 Glue the strips of cardboard to the forehead of the mask. Glue the other pieces to the top of the first strips of cardboard, as shown.

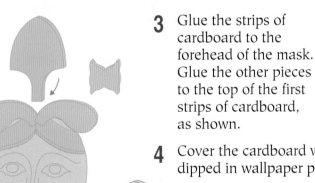

4 Cover the cardboard with strips of newspaper dipped in wallpaper paste. Set aside to dry.

5 Remove the mask from the form. Trim the edges. Make small holes on either side of the eyes for the elastic. Cut out the eye holes, as shown.

6 Paint the mask. Paint the headdress gold. Glue rhinestones to the headdress.

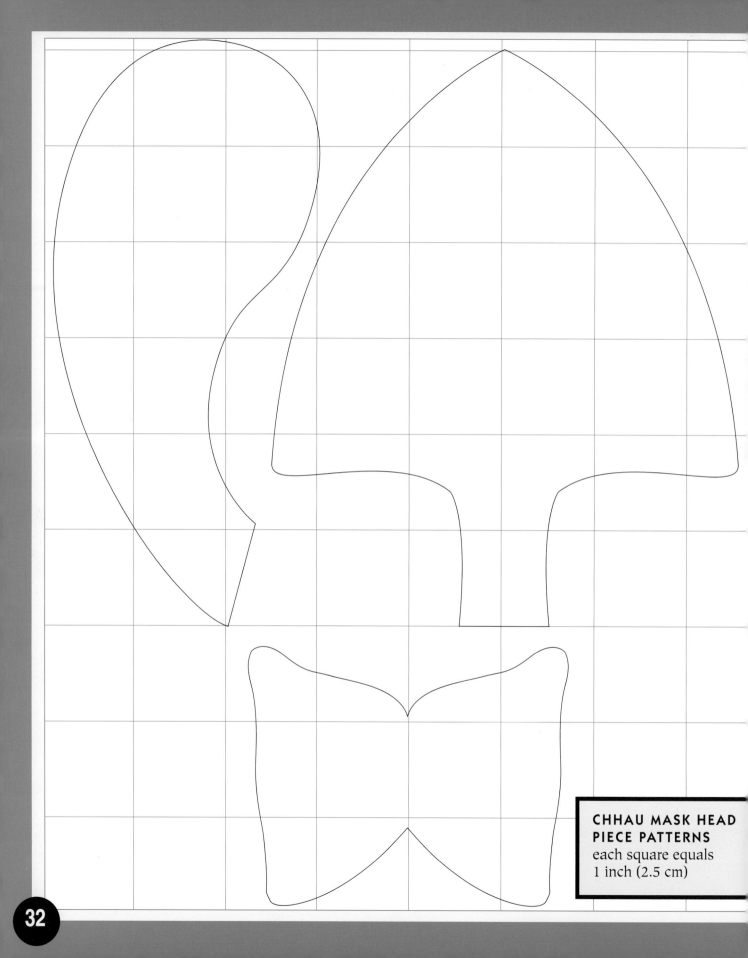

CHHAU MASK HEAD
PIECE PATTERNS
each square equals
1 inch (2.5 cm)

THAI DEMON

MASKS

*These **Khon** masks are based on the masks used in classical Thai masked pantomine. The dancers wear the masks and perform with movements similar to shadow puppets, keeping in profile as much as possible. This style of theater dates back to the 16th century. Thai dance-drama traditions are taught today in Bangkok and plays are performed by the Thai National Theater.*

TECHNIQUE Basic Thai mask

MATERIALS 26 in (66 cm) x 22 in (56 in) flexible light poster board • ruler • pencil • scissors • craft glue • masking tape • newspaper • box of wallpaper paste • water • 1 gallon (4 *l*) pail • paint • metallic gold paint • white rhinestones (optional)

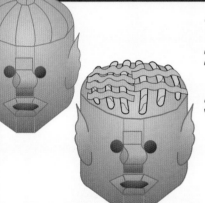

1 Make a basic Thai mask, p9. Do not paint or decorate yet.

2 Make ridges along the top of the head using newspaper sheets twisted into a rope. Attach with strips of newspaper and wallpaper paste, as shown.

3 Make little balls of paper by dipping strips of paper into wallpaper paste and crumpling into balls, as shown. Press the balls against the plastic-covered work surface to make one flat side. Spread a little paste on the flat side of the ball and press in place against the head.

4 Make many little balls and arrange them in rows around the forehead, as shown.

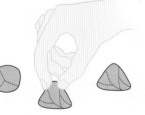

5 Set aside to dry for several days. The small balls on the head take longer to dry than most projects. If any of the balls fall off before they are dry, glue them back in place with craft glue.

6 When the project is dry, paint. Thai masks are very brightly painted with many colors and with gold paint on the head, as shown. If desired, glue white rhinestones on the gold headdress.

TECHNIQUE Basic Thai mask

MATERIALS 26 in (66 cm) x 22 in (56 in) flexible light poster board • ruler • pencil • scissors • craft glue • masking tape • newspaper • box of wallpaper paste • water • 1 gallon (4 *l*) pail • wrapping paper or paper towel cardboard tube • paint • metallic gold paint • white rhinestones (optional)

1 Make a basic Thai mask, p9. Do not paint or decorate yet.

2 To make the tall headdress, cut a wrapping paper or paper towel cardboard tube, as show

3 Using the remaining section of poster board, measure and cut a piece, as shown. Roll into a cone. Overlap the edges, as shown. Glue and tape together.

4 Make cuts in both ends of the cone, as shown.

5 Slide the cone over the tube and position it in the center. Fold the tabs onto the tube and tape in place, as shown.

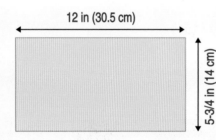

12 in (30.5 cm)

12 in (30.5 cm)

5-3/4 in (14 cm)

4 in (10 cm)

2 in (5 cm)

3/4 in (2 cm)

3/4 in (2 cm)

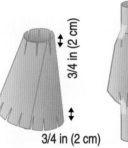

6 Cut another piece of poster board, as shown. Roll into a cone so that it is very tight at one end, as shown. Glue and tape to hold in shape.

7 Trim the wide end of the cone and make cuts in this end, as shown.

8 Place the cone over the end of the cardboard tube, as shown. Bend the tabs onto the tube. Glue and tape in place.

9 Make cuts in the other end of the tube, as shown. Fold the tabs back. Place the tube on top of the mask in the center. Glue and tape the tabs in place.

10 Twist and crumple newspaper sheets into "ropes." Wrap these ropes around the base of the tube to make a more cone-shaped crown on the head, as shown. Tape in place.

7 in (18 cm)

4-1/2 in (11.5 cm)

1 in (2.5 cm)

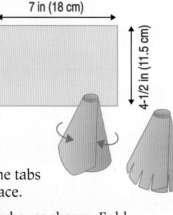

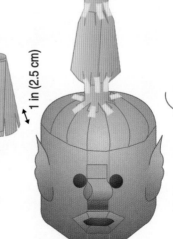

11 Using more newspaper strips and wallpaper paste, cover the headdress and where it joins the mask head with 2 to 3 layers of newspaper strips. Be sure to attach the headdress securely with newspaper strips and wallpaper paste.

12 Make little balls of paper by dipping strips of paper into paste and crumpling into balls. Press the balls against the plastic-covered work surface to make one flat side. Spread a little paste on the flat side of the ball and press in place against the head.

13 Make many little balls and arrange them in rows around the head and headdress, as shown.

14 Set aside to dry for several days. The small balls on the head take longer to dry than most projects. If any of the balls fall off before they are dry, glue them back in place with craft glue.

15 When the project is dry, paint. Thai masks are very brightly painted with many colors and with gold paint on the head, as shown. You may also glue white rhinestones on the headdress, if desired.

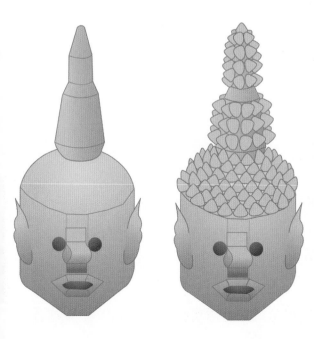

Masks for Disguise

For centuries people have used masks to disguise themselves for special occasions. The basis of the masks and their part in the celebration often had magical or spiritual roots that had been forgotten with only the festivities remaining. Halloween, for example, is now mainly an occasion for parties, games, and fun for children, and does not involve the celebration of All Saints' Day or the Day of the Dead. In some cultures it was believed that spirits of the dead revisited earth and that special occasion connected the event with ghosts and skeletons which are now part of today's Halloween costumes. Other creatures from myths about Dracula and werewolves have also become associated with Halloween. However, dressing up is not limited to supernatural creatures, and children today disguise themselves as anything their imagination desires.

For dressing up, face painting is now popular with children and is used instead of a mask. With the addition of a costume and a wig or hat, the disguise is complete. Face painting disguises are easy to do but require special paint.

MAN AND BOWLER HAT

MASK

TECHNIQUE Basic paper sheet mask with alterations

MATERIALS 8-1/2 x 11 in (21.5 x 30 cm) sheet of bond paper or stiff paper or flexible poster board • ruler • pencil • scissors • paper hole punch • craft glue • masking tape • 1—7 in (18 cm) diameter paper plate • 1—6 in (15 cm) diameter paper bowl • paint or markers • 12 in (30 cm) elastic cord

1 Make a basic paper sheet mask, p6, noting the following alterations. Draw a chin along the bottom of the sheet, and cut out.

2 Draw a line horizontally across the sheet. Fold along this line and make cuts along the top of the mask, up to the fold mark, as shown.

3 To make the bowler hat, glue the paper bowl upside down to the bottom of the plate, as shown.

4 Glue the tabs along the top of the mask to the underside of the hat. Bend the top of the mask in a slight curve, and place the front of the mask in from the edge of the plate, as shown. Tape in place until the glue dries. Remove all tape.

5 Paint and decorate. Attach the elastic cord, see p6.

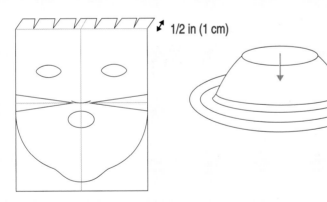

1/2 in (1 cm)

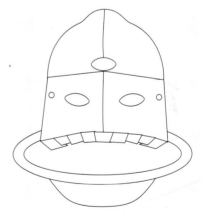

TECHNIQUE Basic paper sheet mask with alterations

MATERIALS 8-1/2 x 11 in (21.5 x 30 cm) sheet of bond paper or stiff paper or flexible poster board • ruler • pencil • scissors • paper hole punch • craft glue • masking tape • 2—10 in (25.5 cm) diameter paper plates • paint or markers • 12 in (30 cm) elastic cord

WITCH

MASK

1. Make a basic paper sheet mask, p6, with the following alterations. Draw a chin and hair along the bottom of the sheet and cut out along the lines.

2. Draw a line horizontally across the sheet, as shown. Fold along this line and make cuts along the top of the mask, up to the fold mark, as shown.

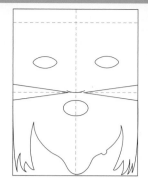
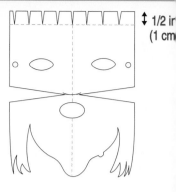

1/2 in (1 cm)

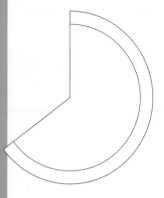
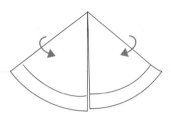
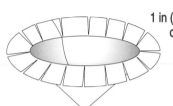

1 in (2.5 cm) cuts

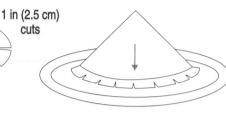

3. To make the witch's hat cut out one-third of one of the paper plates, as shown, and discard.

4. Using the remaining piece, overlap the cuts making a cone, and glue. Tape to hold in place until the glue dries.

5. Make cuts around the open end of the cone, as shown.

6. Fold the tabs back and glue to the bottom of the other plate, as shown.

7. Glue the tabs along the top of the mask to the underside of the hat. Bend the top of the mask in a slight curve, and place the front of the mask in from the edge of the plate, as shown. Tape in place until the glue dries. Remove all tape.

8. Paint and decorate. Attach the elastic cord, see p6 for instructions.

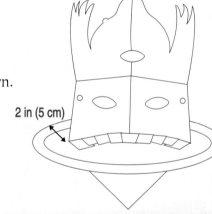

2 in (5 cm)

WEREWOLF

MASK

TECHNIQUE Basic paper sheet mask

MATERIALS 8-1/2 x 11 in (21.5 x 30 cm) shee of bond paper or stiff paper or flexible poste board • ruler • pencil • scissors • paper hol punch • craft glue • masking tape • paint o markers • 12 in (30 cm) elastic cord

1. To make the werewolf mask, make a basic paper sheet mask, p6.

2. Draw 2 pointed ears on each side of the mask. Cut around the ears.

3. Trim the rest of the edges of the mask to look like fur.

Paint and decorate. Attach the elastic cord, see p6.

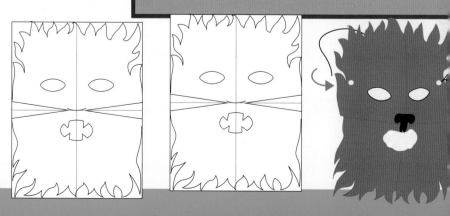

MAN AND BRIM HAT

TECHNIQUE Basic paper plate mask

MATERIALS 1—10 in (25.5 cm) paper plate • 1—7 in (23 cm) paper plate • ruler • pencil • scissors • sheet of heavy paper • paper hole punch • craft glue • masking tape • paint or markers • 12 in (30 cm) elastic cord

MASK

1 Using the large paper plate, make a basic paper plate mask, p8.

2 To make the brim for the hat, cut the small paper plate in half.

3 Cut the flat side of one piece in an arch to fit the top of the large plate, as shown. Glue this piece above the face.

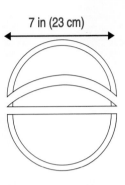

7 in (23 cm)

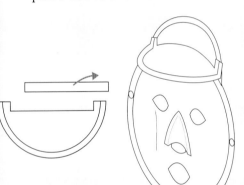

4 Cut out a center notch from the other half, as shown, leaving a paper plate tab on either side.

5 Glue this half across the top of the face to make a brim.

6 Paint and decorate. Attach the elastic cord, see p6.

OLD LADY

MASK

TECHNIQUE Basic papier-mâché strip mask

MATERIALS plastic-covered styrofoam head form or plastic-covered ball of newspaper (p7) • newspaper • ruler • 1 gallon (4 *l*) pail • measuring cups • box of wallpaper paste • water • plastic wrap • plasticine • 12 in (30 cm) elastic cord • scissors • paint • artificial hair or yarn

1 Make a basic papier-mâché strip mask, p8.

2 Spread a half sheet of newspaper with wallpaper paste. Lay another sheet over it and smooth in place.

3 Tear pieces of the wet double sheet to desired size, and lay the pieces over the wet mask form. Bunch the sheet into wrinkles. Make the wrinkles fold horizontally across the forehead. Make small wrinkles fanning out from the outside corners of the eyes, and make deeper vertical folds along the side of the mouth. Cover the cheeks, nose, and chin with shallower, bunched wrinkles, as shown.

4 Set aside in a warm place to dry. When dry, paint.

5 Attach artificial hair or yarn to head with glue. Attach the elastic cord, see p8.

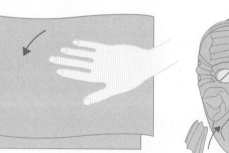

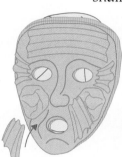

TECHNIQUE Basic papier-mâché pulp mask

MATERIALS plastic-covered styrofoam head form or plastic-covered ball of newspaper (p7) • newspaper • ruler • 1 gallon (4 *l*) pail • measuring cups • box of wallpaper paste • water • plastic wrap • plasticine • scissors • table knife • artificial hair or yarn • glue • paint • 12 in (30 cm) elastic cord

OLD MAN

MASK

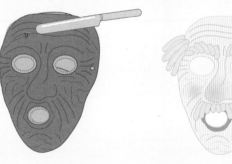

1 Working on a plastic-covered work surface, make a basic papier-mâché pulp mask, p7.

2 Make a small hole in the papier-mâché pulp on each side of the mask at the same level as the eyes, as shown.

3 Model the face so that the nose is large, and the surface is wrinkled. Use a table knife to make ridges in the pulp. Make the creases run horizontally across the forehead. Make small creases fanning out from the outside corners of the eyes, and make deeper vertical lines along the side of the mouth.

4 Set aside in a warm place to dry. When dry, paint.

5 Attach artificial hair or yarn to head with glue.

6 Attach the elastic cord, see p7.

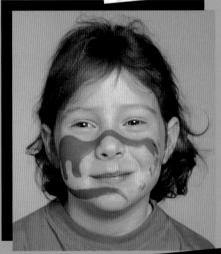

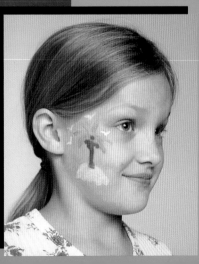

Face painting
top to bottom—
Dinosaur 1, p42
Dinosaur 2, p42
Rose, p46
Island, p46

41

DINOSAURS

FACE PAINTING

TECHNIQUE Cheek art

TECHNIQUE Cheek art

MATERIALS water-based face paints: green, blue, black • paint brush • headband • tissues • cotton swabs

1 See p11 for basic face painting techniques.

2 Using green, paint a dinosaur shape on the cheek, as shown.

3 Using blue, paint triangles along the spine of the dinosaur. Use the black paint to paint an eye.

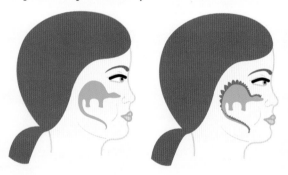

TECHNIQUE Whole face painting

MATERIALS water-based face paints: green, black • paint brush • headband • tissues • cotton swabs

2

1 See p11 for basic face painting techniques.

2 Using green, draw a dinosaur body on one cheek. Draw a long neck over the bridge of the nose, and a head on the opposite cheek. Draw a long tail along the jaw and over the chin, as shown.

3 Fill the shape with green paint.

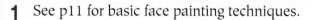

LEOPARD

FACE PAINTING

TECHNIQUE Whole face painting

MATERIALS water-based face paints: white, black, yellow ochre • paint brush • headband • tissues • cotton swabs

1 See p11 for basic face painting techniques.

2 Draw a white line around the mouth and chin, beginning at one side of the nose. Draw down one side, under the chin, and back up to the other side of the nose. Fill in the circle with white. Do not color the lips.

3 With black, draw arched black eyebrows, as shown. Color the end of the nose black right down to the upper lip. Draw 2 arches across the cheek, as shown.

4 With black, draw semi-circles 1/2 in (1 cm) in diameter. Leave the cheek area clear.

5 With yellow ochre, draw spots inside each black semi-circle. Color the bridge of the nose yellow ochre, as well.

6 Draw black whiskers across the cheek area. Add rows of small black dots across the white chin.

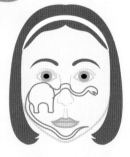

4 Draw plants for the dinosaur to eat on the other cheek. Use the black paint to make an eye.

BUTTERFLY

FACE PAINTING

> **TECHNIQUE** Whole face painted
>
> **MATERIALS** water-based face paints: orange, white, turquoise, blue, green, black • paint brush • headband • tissues • cotton swabs

1 See p11 for basic face painting techniques.

2 Using the orange paint, draw butterfly wing shapes centering the butterfly along the nose. Draw circles around the eyes, and in the corners of the wing shapes, as shown.

3 Fill in the wing shapes with orange. Fill the circles with white.

4 Using the blue paint, paint circles inside the smaller white circles, as shown.

5 Paint black outlines around the white circles. Paint a butterfly body, head, and antennae in the center of the butterfly.

6 Using the turquoise paint, draw a wavy line around the outside of each wing, as shown.

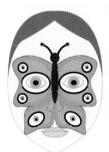

TECHNIQUES Cut-out paper beak and whole face painted

MATERIALS yellow construction paper • scissors • glue • 12 in (30 cm) elastic cord • water-based face paints: white, blue, red, green, black • paint brush • make-up sponge • headband • tissues • cotton swabs

1 See p11 for basic face painting techniques.

2 To make the beak, cut out a beak shape from yellow construction paper using the pattern provided. Overlap the tabs where indicated, and glue.

3 Poke a hole on each side of the beak just above the over-lapped area, as shown. Tie the elastic cord through one hole.

4 Place the beak against the face and determine the correct length for the elastic. Tie the elastic through the hole, and cut off any excess.

5 To paint the face, use white paint, color a heavy white outline around each eye. Make the outside of the outline extend toward the temples, as shown.

6 Paint the forehead blue and extend the blue color down onto the bridge of the nose.

7 Draw feather shapes from the corner of the nose across the cheek to the jaw line. Color the cheeks with red from the feather shapes up to the white eye rings.

8 Paint the temples and the chin with green.

9 With black paint, draw feather shapes across the red areas. Put on the beak.

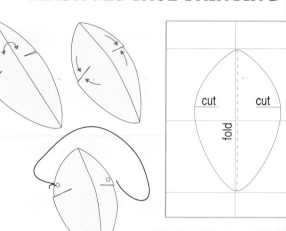

BEAK PATTERN
each square equals 1 inch (2.5 cm)

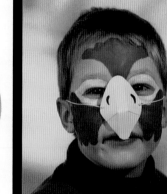

TECHNIQUES Cut-out paper ears and whole face painting

MATERIALS poster board • pencil • scissors • glue • masking tape • paint • rigid black headband • water-based face paints: white, black • paint brush • make-up sponge • headband • tissues • cotton swabs

1 See p11 for basic face painting techniques.

2 To make the ears, transfer the pattern (p45) onto the poster board. Cut out.

3 Make the cut in the center of the ear where indicated. Fold the side tabs were indicated.

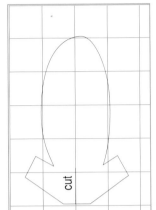

EAR PATTERN
each square equals
1 inch (2.5 cm)

cut

3 Overlap the center section, as shown. Glue in place.

4 Cut out two pieces of poster board, as shown.
Glue one piece to each side of the ear, as shown.

5 Make another ear. Reverse the pattern on the poster board so that the ear curves in the opposite direction. Assemble in the same way.

6 Paint the ears, as shown.

7 Place one ear on top of the headband, off center so that the ear curves inward, as shown. Bend the tabs around the band and tape underneath.

8 Attach the other ear in the same way on the other side of the headband.

1 in (2.5 cm)

2 in (5 cm)

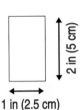

9 To paint the face, use white paint, draw a line across the bridge of the nose. Continue the line down the side of the nose and across the cheek. Using the make-up sponge, paint the entire face white above this line.

10 Using black, paint the area below the white.

11 Using black, paint a line down the center of the nose between the eyes. Paint arched lines over the top of the first line.

12 Continue to paint black lines over the top of the forehead, as shown. As you get closer to the hairline, make the lines wider, and more wavy.

13 Paint black lines across the cheek, as shown.

14 Paint black lines across the other cheek, mirroring the design on the opposite side as much as possible.

15 Put on the ears.

ISLAND

FACE PAINTING

TECHNIQUE Cheek art

MATERIALS water-based face paints: yellow, light green, dark green, brown, blue, white • paint brush • headband • tissues • cotton swabs

1 See p11 for basic face painting techniques.

2 Using yellow, paint a semi-circle on the lower part of the cheek. Using the light green, paint palm leaf shapes above the yellow semi-circle. Using dark green, draw lines along each leaf shape.

3 Using brown, paint a curved trunk connecting the leaves and the yellow island. Paint brown circles at the top of the trunk for coconuts.

4 Using blue, draw waves around the island. Use white to draw seagulls above the palm tree.

ROSE

FACE PAINTING

TECHNIQUE Cheek art

MATERIALS water-based face paints: white, pink, yellow, green • paint brush • headband • tissues • cotton swabs

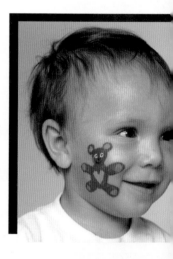

1 See p11 for basic face painting techniques.

2 Using white paint, draw a flower with 5 petals on the cheek. Make the petals flat or slightly concave across the tip. Fill in with white.

3 Paint green leaves around the white flower.

4 Paint a yellow center in the middle of the flower. Make pink lines along the petals, as shown.

TEDDY BEAR
FACE PAINTING

TECHNIQUE Cheek art

MATERIALS water-based face paints: white, pink, yellow, green • paint brush • headband • tissues • cotton swabs

1 See p11 for basic face painting techniques.

2 Using brown paint, draw an oval shape for the bear's body. Draw a circle above the oval for a head. Draw 4 ovals for legs, and 2 circles for ears. Do not color in the shapes.

3 Paint pink circles at the end of each leg, and in the center of the ears. Paint a pink heart in the middle of the body.

4 Fill the body shapes with brown, painting around the pink shapes.

5 Paint 2 yellow circles for eyes. Make a black dot in the center of each circle. Make a black circle for a nose, and 2 curved black lines for the mouth.

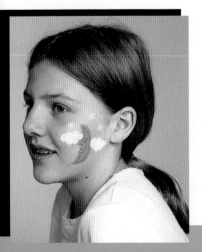

CELESTIAL
FACE PAINTING

TECHNIQUE Cheek art

MATERIALS water-based face paints: orange, pale yellow • paint brush • headband • tissues • cotton swabs

1

1 See p11 for basic face painting techniques.

2 Using orange, draw a circle in the center of the cheek. Draw rays around the outside of the circle, as shown.

3 Fill the rays and circles with pale yellow. Draw another line of rays inside the first line of rays.

4 Draw an orange face in the center of the circle.

TECHNIQUE Cheek art

MATERIALS water-based face paints: pale blue, dark blue, white, yellow • paint brush • headband • tissues • cotton swabs

2

1 See p11 for basic face painting techniques.

2 Using pale blue, paint a moon shape in the center of the cheek.

3 Using dark blue, paint a face on the shape. Draw a dark blue line around the outside of the moon.

4 Using yellow, paint stars above the moon. Using white, paint clouds overlapping the moon.

Masked Balls

Adults also enjoy disguises and use them to walk in parades or attend masked balls. Balls were especially popular during the 18th century. Beautiful and elaborate masks, many covering only the top half of the face, were tied behind the head, attached to a hat, or held in front of the face by a stick.

Carnival, a pre-Lent festivity, is celebrated in many countries. In the United States it climaxes with the Mardi Gras season with parades and costumes. It is particularly popular in New Orleans. In Rio de Janeiro, modern carnival is celebrated with masked balls, parades, elaborate costumes, and other special festivities.

BIRD OF PARADISE

HALF MASK

> **TECHNIQUE** Basic papier-mâché pulp mask
>
> **MATERIALS** styrofoam head form or plastic-covered ball of newspaper (p7) • newspaper • ruler • 1 gallon (4 *l*) pail • measuring cups • box of wallpaper paste • water • plastic wrap • plasticine • pencil • fine sandpaper • paint • feathers (available at craft supply stores) • 12 in (30 cm) elastic cord • scissors

1 On a plastic-covered work surface, make a basic papier-mâché pulp mask, p7. Build up the pulp to approximately 1/2 in (1 cm) thick. Model the top of the head simple and rounded. Model the beak area over plasticine that is arched, as shown, making the tip pointed. The cheek area is modeled in feather shapes. Make an outline of raised pulp around each eye. Use a pencil to make small holes where the feathers will be inserted across the forehead.

2 Make a small hole in the pulp on each side of the mask at the same level as the eyes for the elastic cord that holds the mask on.

3 Set aside in a warm dry place to harden. Papier mâché may take several days to dry, depending on thickness, moisture content, and humidity.

4 When dry, the mask may be removed from the plasticine form. If a smooth surface is desired, sand the mask.

5 Paint the mask in the colors desired.

6 Insert the feathers into the holes made earlier and glue in place.

7 Attach the elastic cord to the sides of the mask, see p7.

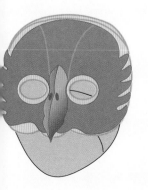

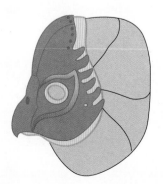

HARLEQUIN

HALF MASK

1 On a plastic-covered work surface, make a basic papier-mâché pulp mask, p7. Build up the pulp to approximately 1/2 in (1 cm) thick. Model the forehead simple and rounded. The cheek area extends back almost to the ear, as shown. Make a ridge of pulp over the eyes for eyebrows. Make 2 teardrop shapes under each eye.

TECHNIQUE Basic papier-mâché pulp mask

MATERIALS styrofoam head form or plastic-covered ball of newspaper (p7) • newspaper • ruler • 1 gallon (4 l) pail • measuring cups • box of wallpaper paste • water • plastic wrap • plasticine • pencil • fine sandpaper • paint • 12 in (30 cm) elastic cord • scissors • glitter

CAT

HALF MASK

TECHNIQUE Basic papier-mâché pulp mask

MATERIALS styrofoam head form or plastic-covered ball of newspaper (p7) • newspaper • ruler • 1 gallon (4 l) pail • measuring cups • box of wallpaper paste • water • plastic wrap • plasticine • pencil • fine sandpaper • paint • 16—12 in (30 cm) long chenille stems • 12 in (30 cm) elastic cord • scissors

1 On a plastic-covered work surface, make a basic papier-mâché pulp mask, p7. The pulp should be built up to approximately 1/2 in (1 cm) thick. Model pointed ears at the top of the mask. Model the nose in a slightly scooped shape, with a narrow bridge and a blunt end, as shown.

2 Build up the cheek areas very close to the nose using extra pulp made into round balls, as shown.

3 Model the nose with a flat end and rounded sides. With a pencil, make a groove down the center of the end and poke the pulp with the pencil to make long nostrils on each side of the groove, as shown.

4 Use the pencil to make small holes in the cheek area. These are for the whiskers. Make 16 holes in each cheek.

5 Make a small hole in the pulp on each side of the mask at the same level as the eyes for the elastic cord that holds the mask on.

2 Make a small hole in the pulp on each side of the mask at the same level as the eyes for the elastic cord that holds the mask on.

3 Set aside in a warm dry place to harden. Papier-mâché may take several days to dry, depending on thickness, moisture content, and humidity.

4 When dry, the mask may be removed from the plasticine form. If a smooth surface is desired, sand the mask.

5 Paint the mask in the colors desired. Add glitter where desired.

6 Attach the elastic cord to the sides of the mask, see p7.

6 Set aside in a warm dry place to harden. Papier mâché may take several days to dry, depending on thickness, moisture content, and humidity.

7 When dry, the mask may be removed from the plasticine form. If a smooth surface is desired, sand the mask. Paint the mask.

8 Cut the chenille stems in half. Glue one piece in each hole in the cheek areas.

9 Attach the elastic cord in the side holes, see p7.

SUN
HALF MASK

TECHNIQUE Basic paper plate mask

MATERIALS 1—10 in (25.5 cm) paper plate • ruler • pencil • paper hole punch • craft glue • masking tape • paint • 12 in (30 cm) elastic cord • scissors

TECHNIQUE Basic papier-mâché pulp mask

MATERIALS styrofoam head form or plastic-covered ball of newspaper (p7) • newspaper • ruler • 1 gallon (4 l) pail • measuring cups • box of wallpaper paste • water • plastic wrap • plasticine • pencil • fine sandpaper • paint • white feathers (available at craft supply stores) • 12 in (30 cm) elastic cord • scissors

SWAN
HALF MASK

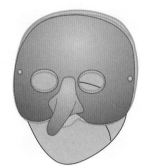

1. On a plastic-covered work surface, make a basic papier-mâché pulp mask, p7. Build up the pulp to approximately 1/2 in (1 cm) thick. Model the top of the head simple and rounded. Model the beak area over plasticine, as shown, making the end slightly rounded.

2. Make a small hole in the pulp on each side of the mask at the same level as the eyes for the elastic cord that holds the mask on.

3. Set aside in a warm dry place to harden. Papier mâché may take several days to dry, depending on thickness, moisture content, and humidity.

4. When dry, the mask may be removed from the plasticine form. If a smooth surface is desired, sand the mask.

5. Paint the mask white, the beak orange, and the eyes and forehead areas white.

1 Make a basic paper plate mask, p9.

2 Turn the plate bottom side up. In the center of the plate, draw eyes to fit the wearer, as described on p4 (Proportions).

3 Draw around the nose area, as shown.

4 Around the top of plate draw rays, as shown.

5 Cut out around the drawn outline and the eye shapes.

6 Paint and decorate.

7 Attach the elastic cord, see p6.

6 Glue white feathers over the white areas of the mask. Start at the outside edge of the mask, and glue the feathers in a row, as shown. Continue toward the beak, gluing feathers in rows, overlapping the previous row, until the white areas of the mask are covered.

7 Attach the elastic cord in the side holes, see p7.

Carnivals

Carnivals were originally associated with Lent, a final festivity before the 40-day pre-Lent observances. Carnival celebrations vary in each country but usually involve music, costume, and dance. Carnival celebrations are popular and carnival has influenced the development of popular theater, folk dance, and popular song.

CHINESE DRAGON

MASK

1 To make the mask shell, follow basic papier-mâché strip mask over a balloon, p8.

2 Cut an opening large enough to allow the balloon to fit over the head. The top of the shell should rest on the top of the head.

3 Mark the position of the eyes, but do not cut. Draw an opening around the eyes, as shown, and cut out.

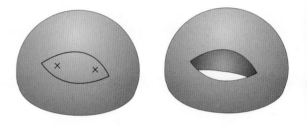

4 Using the pattern on p57, draw the upper lip shape on corrugated cardboard. Cut out. Curl the shape into an arc, and glue or tape in place above the eye opening.

5 Using the pattern on p56, draw a cheek shape on corrugated cardboard. Cut out. Glue the cheek shape against the side of the head, overlapping the upper lip shape, as shown.

6 Draw and cut out a second cheek shape and glue to the opposite side of the head in the same way.

7 Using the pattern on p57, draw the chin shape on corrugated cardboard. Cut out. Bend the shape in a curve, and glue the ends of the chin shape to the inside of the ends of the cheek shapes, as shown.

8 Using the pattern on p57, draw the forehead shape on corrugated cardboard. Cut out. Curl the shape into an arc, and glue or tape in place on top of the shell.

UPPER LIP   **CHEEK**   **CHIN**   **FOREHEAD**

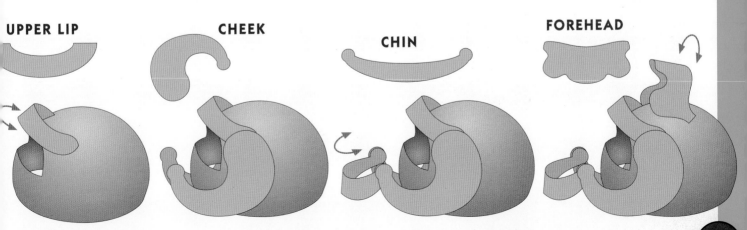

9 Cut strips of corrugated cardboard 1 to 2 in (2.5 to 5 cm) wide, and long enough to cover the bottom of the jaw. Bend one end of a strip, and place against the inside of a cheek piece Place the other end of the strip against the opposite side of the jaw, bending the end to fit in place. Trim if necessary, and glue both ends in place.

10 Using the pattern on p56, draw the tongue shape on corrugated cardboard. Cut out. Bend into a curve, and glue to the front of the shell, just below the opening.

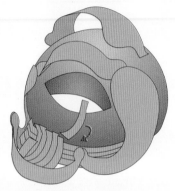

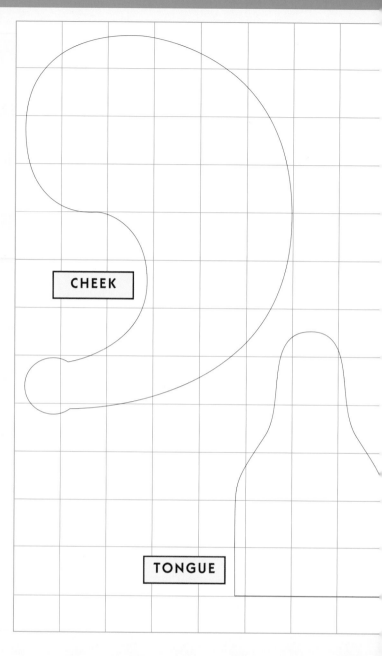

CHEEK

TONGUE

11 Crumple sheets of newspaper and fill the spaces beneath the upper lip piece and the forehead piece. Tape in place. Crumple a double sheet of newspaper into a ball about 3 in (7.5 cm) in diameter. Tape the ball to hold its shape. Glue the ball to the top of the cheek piece for an eye. Make another ball in the same way and glue to the other cheek piece. Make 4 smaller balls from half sheets of newspaper in the same way. Glue 2 of the smaller balls to the upper lip for nostrils. Glue one small ball to the chin piece where it meets the cheek. Glue the last small ball to the other side of the chin in the same way.

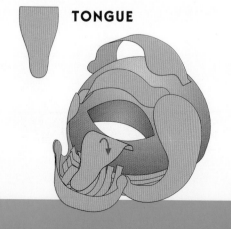

TONGUE

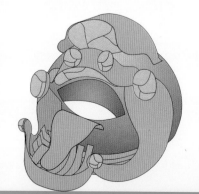

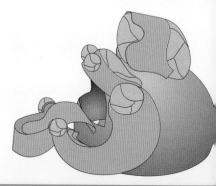

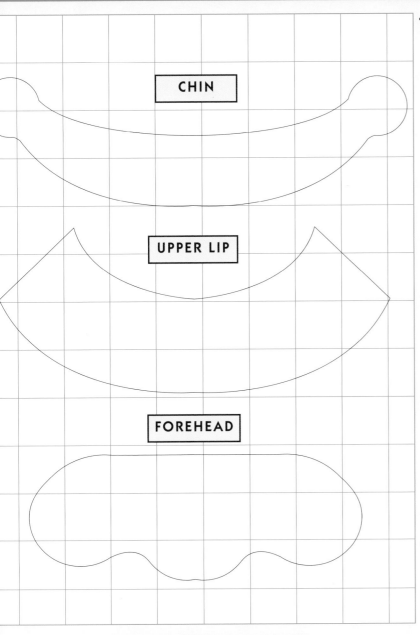

CHIN

UPPER LIP

FOREHEAD

12 Using wire cutters, cut the coat hanger into two straight pieces, 15 in (38 cm) long. Bend each piece of wire into a "S" curve. Roll a double sheet of newspaper into a rope, and tightly twist the rope of paper around one of the wires, taping in place. Add more ropes of newspaper in the same way to completely cover the wire, and make the shape about 1.5 in (3.5 cm) thick. Cover the second wire in the same way, to make 2 horns. Glue the horn to the back of the head, as shown.

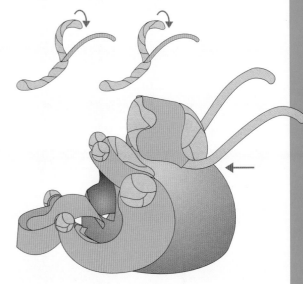

13 Cover all the additions to the shell with strips of paper dipped in wallpaper paste. Set aside to dry. When hard, paint.

CHINESE DRAGON PATTERNS each square equals 1 inch (2.5 cm)

14 Cut out teeth from the poster board and glue to the inside of the mouth. See photograph, p54.

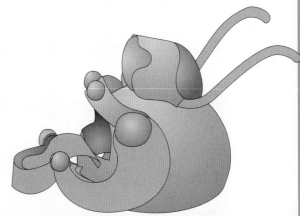

FROG

MASK

This mask is based on a mask used in a Japanese festival.

TECHNIQUE Basic papier-mâché strip mask over a balloon

MATERIALS 9 in (23 cm) balloon • newspaper • ruler • 1 gallon (4 l) pail • measuring cups • box of wallpaper paste • water • string • craft knife • fine sandpaper • pen • craft glue • masking tape • paint • 12 in (30 cm) elastic cord • scissors • 24 in (62 cm) square piece of pink tulle • warm glue gun or epoxy glue

1 To make the mask shell, follow the instructions on page 8.

2 From the wide end of the shell, draw an oval shape, as shown.

3 Cut off the front section of the shell in one piece. The shell should rest comfortably on top of the head of the wearer with the opening beginning above the eyes. If necessary, trim the opening for the correct fit.

6 Using the piece cut off the front, draw a crescent shape, as shown. Cut out this shape. Set aside. This will be the mouth.

7 To make the eyes, crumple a sheet of newspaper into a flattened ball, as shown. Hold the paper in the desired shape with masking tape. Make 2 balls.

8 Tape the paper balls to the top of the shell, one on each side, as shown.

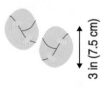

3 in (7.5 cm)

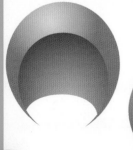

21 in (53 cm)

4 in (10 cm)

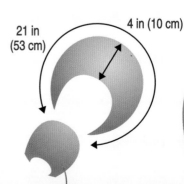

9   Cover the balls with strips of newspaper dipped in wallpaper paste. Set aside to dry.

10 Paint the shell and mouth to resemble a frog. Paint the outside of the head and mouth green, the inside of the head and mouth pink, and the eyes gold. See photo.

11 Punch a small hole in each end of the mouth piece.

12 Punch a hole in the shell on each side of the opening, as shown.

13 Cut the piece of elastic cord in two equal pieces. Thread one end of one of the pieces through the hole in the mouth piece, and knot on the outside, as shown.

14 Place the mouth piece in position in front of the head so that the wide side of the mouth piece is facing up and forward. Thread the other end of the cord through the hole in the side of the head, and knot on the inside.

15 Thread the other piece of cord through the other side of the mouth and attach to the head in the same way.

16 Using a warm glue gun or epoxy glue, attach the pink tulle around the inside of the mouth and head.

17 To put on the mask, swing the mouth section up to enlarge the opening at the neck area and slip the shell over the head. Pull the mouth section down, and arrange the tulle so that it is comfortable in front of the face.

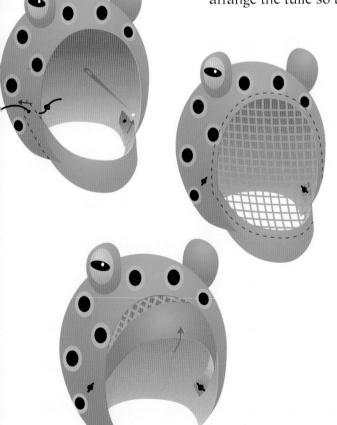

SNOWMAN

MASK

This mask is based on a mask used for Winter Carnival in Montreal.

TECHNIQUE Basic papier-mâché strip mask over a balloon

MATERIALS 12 in (30 cm) balloon • newspaper • ruler • 1 gallon (4 *l*) pail • measuring cups • box of wallpaper paste • water • string • craft knife • fine sandpaper • pen • craft glue • masking tape • paint • scissors • mop head replacement • glitter

1 To make the mask shell, follow instructions on page 8.

2 With a sharp knife *carefully* cut an opening in the open end of the shell, as shown. The top of the shell should rest comfortably on the top of the head of the wearer.

3 Fit the shell over the head to determine where the eye holes and mouth should fall. See p4 (Proportions). Mark the position of the eyes and mouth with a pen. Remove the shell from the head, then draw the eye shapes and mouth shape in place. Cut out the eyes and mouth holes.

4 Crumple a sheet of newspaper into a ball 2 in (5 cm) in diameter. Tape in place for a nose.

5 Lay a double sheet of newspaper flat on the work surface and spread with wallpaper paste. Place another sheet of newspaper on top of the wet sheet and smooth in place. Spread the second sheet with paste and add a third sheet in the same way.

6 Crumple several sheets of newspaper into an oval, as shown. Place the ball in the center of the triple sheet, and roll the wet sheet around the ball, forming a cone. Fold the open end of the cone inward. Place the cone on top of the balloon head.

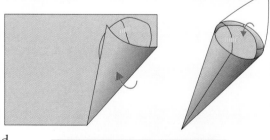

7 Crumple a double sheet of newspaper into a rope. Place it on top of another sheet of newspaper. Fold the sheet over the crumpled paper, and continue to fold the paper over, as shown. Tape the ends together to form a loop.

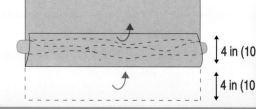

8 Cover this loop with strips of newspaper dipped in wallpaper paste.

9 Place the loop over the cone. Fold the cone over and bunch the end into a ball.

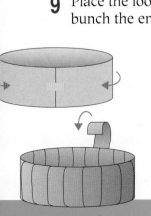

10 Cover the end of the cone and the nose ball with strips of newspaper dipped in wallpaper paste. Set aside to dry.

11 Paint. If desired, sprinkle the head with glitter while the paint is still wet to resemble snow.

MASK

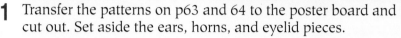

TECHNIQUE Cut pattern mask

MATERIALS 28 x 22 in (71 x 56 cm) sheets of flexible poster board • ruler • pencil • scissors • masking tape • craft glue • paint

NOTE This mask is not recommended for young children where excellent vision is necessary for safety, such as trick-or-treating outside in traffic.

1 Transfer the patterns on p63 and 64 to the poster board and cut out. Set aside the ears, horns, and eyelid pieces.

2 Draw the dotted line around the edge of the two side pieces, as shown on the pattern.

3 Make cuts up to the dotted line all around the side pieces, as shown.

4 Lay one of the side pieces flat on the table and bend tabs upward.

5 Using the long, narrow pattern strip and starting under the chin, glue the strip to one side piece by spreading glue on a few tabs at a time. Then wrap the long narrow strip around the side piece, working towards the back of the cow's head, as shown. Press the strip against the tabs with glue. If the glue doesn't hold immediately, use masking tape to hold in place until dry.

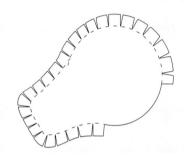
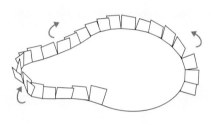
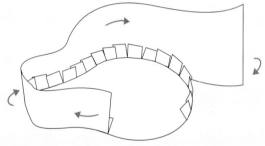

6 Lay the other side piece on the table, facing the opposite direction as the head, and bend the tabs on the second side piece upward, as shown.

7 Turn this side piece over, and fit it into the open side of the head, as shown. Starting under the chin as before, spread glue on a few of the tabs and press in place against the long strip. Press the tabs in place from the inside of the mask. If necessary, hold in place with tape until the glue dries.

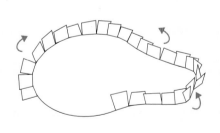
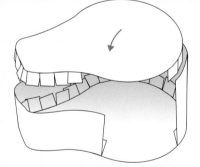
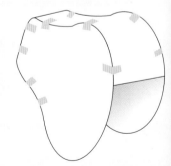

8 The long strip should stop at the back of the mask, leaving an opening large enough to go over the head of the wearer. If necessary, enlarge this opening to fit by cutting away some of the end of the narrow strip.

9 Draw the eyes and mouth as measured for wearer (see p4). Carefully cut out with a craft knife. The eyes are cut across the seam of the head. Because the eye holes of this mask are not close to the eyes of the wearer, they must be quite large to allow the wearer to see. Make sure that the mouth is large enough for the wearer to see the floor in front of his or her feet. Check to make sure the wearer can move around safely.

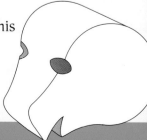

62

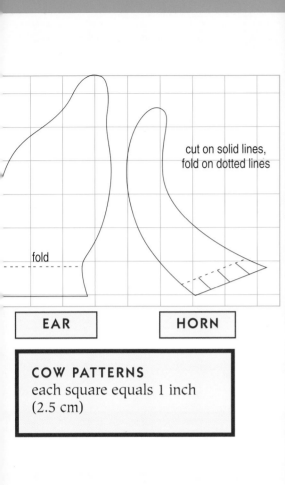

cut on solid lines,
fold on dotted lines

fold

EAR   **HORN**

COW PATTERNS
each square equals 1 inch
(2.5 cm)

10 To attach the ears to the head, bend the tab at the base of each ear. Glue one ear to each side of the head, as shown.

11 Make cuts in the end of each horn piece, as shown. Bend these tabs back and glue them to the top of the head. Bend the base of the horn in a gentle curve, overlapping the tabs, as shown. Tape in place until the glue dries.

12 To make eyelids, make cuts very close together along the bottom edge, as shown. Bend the eyelid pieces in an arch, and glue one over each eye.

13 When all the glued parts are dry, remove the masking tape and paint.

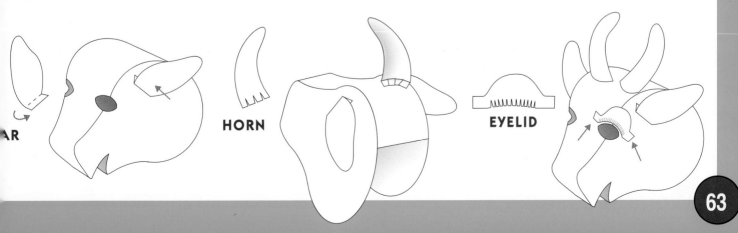

AR   **HORN**   **EYELID**

63

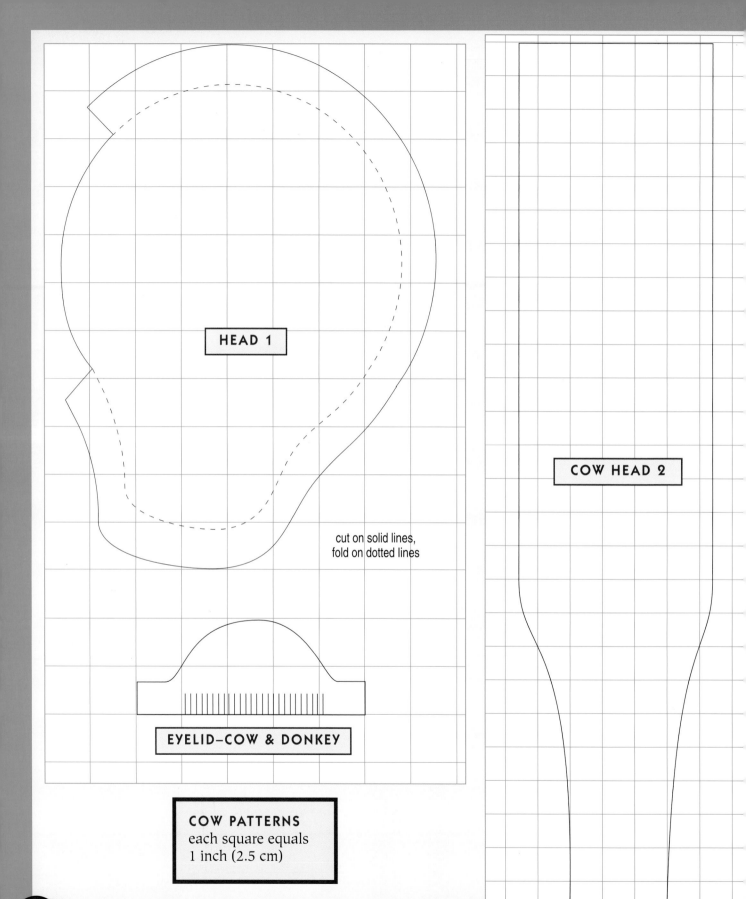

HEAD 1

cut on solid lines,
fold on dotted lines

COW HEAD 2

EYELID—COW & DONKEY

COW PATTERNS
each square equals
1 inch (2.5 cm)

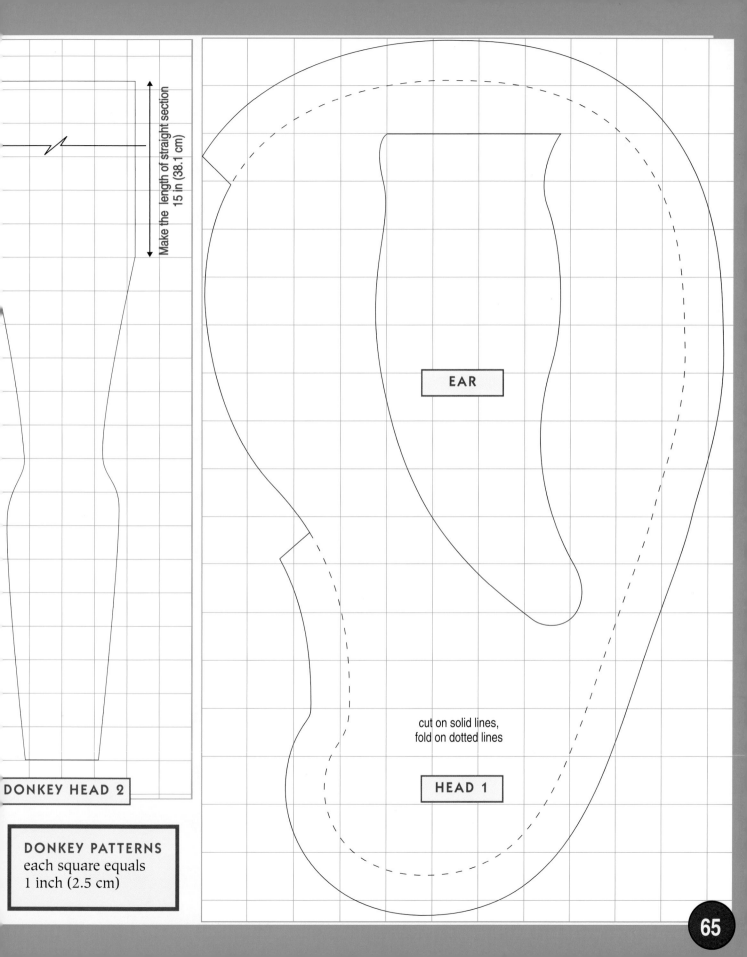

Make the length of straight section
15 in (38.1 cm)

DONKEY HEAD 2

DONKEY PATTERNS
each square equals
1 inch (2.5 cm)

EAR

cut on solid lines,
fold on dotted lines

HEAD 1

DONKEY

A Midsummer Night's Dream MASK

> **TECHNIQUE** Cut pattern mask
>
> **MATERIALS** 28 x 22 in (71 x 56 cm) sheets of flexible poster board • ruler • pencil • scissors • craft glue • masking tape • paint • artificial flowers and vines • florist's wire

1 Transfer the eyelid pattern on p64 and the other pattern pieces on p65 to the poster board and cut out. Set aside the ear and eyelid pieces.

2 To construct and assemble the donkey head mask, follow steps 2 through 9 of the cow head mask, p62.

3 To attach the ears to the head, overlap tabs at the base of each ear. Glue one ear to each side of the head, as shown.

4 To make eyelids, make cuts very close together along the bottom edge, as shown. Bend the eyelid pieces in an arch, and glue one over each eye.

5 When all the glued parts are dry, remove the masking tape and paint.

6 Make a crown of flowers by wrapping stems of artificial flowers and vines together with the florist's wire. Make the rope of flowers long enough to wrap around the top of the donkey's head.

7 Wrap the rope around the head and wire the ends together.

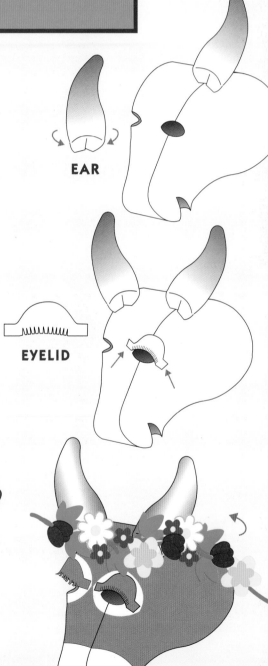

EAR

EYELID

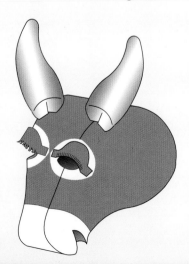

TECHNIQUE Cut pattern mask

MATERIALS poster board • corrugated cardboard • newspaper • 1 gallon (4 *l*) pail • measuring cups • box of wallpaper paste • water • ruler • pencil • scissors • table knife • glue • tape • paint

DEER

MASK

1 Cut a strip of poster board long enough to wrap around the forehead and overlap 1 in (2.5 cm). Wrap the strip around the head, as shown. Overlap the ends and glue together. Tape in place until glue dries.

2 Cut another strip of posterboard long enough to cross the top of head. Glue one end of the second strip to the strip wrapped around the head. Bend the second strip over the head and glue to the other side of the forehead strip.

3 Cut another strip of posterboard and attach to the forehead strip in the same way, crossing the head in a different direction, as shown.

4 Add more strips in the same way, forming a stiff cap. Remove from head.

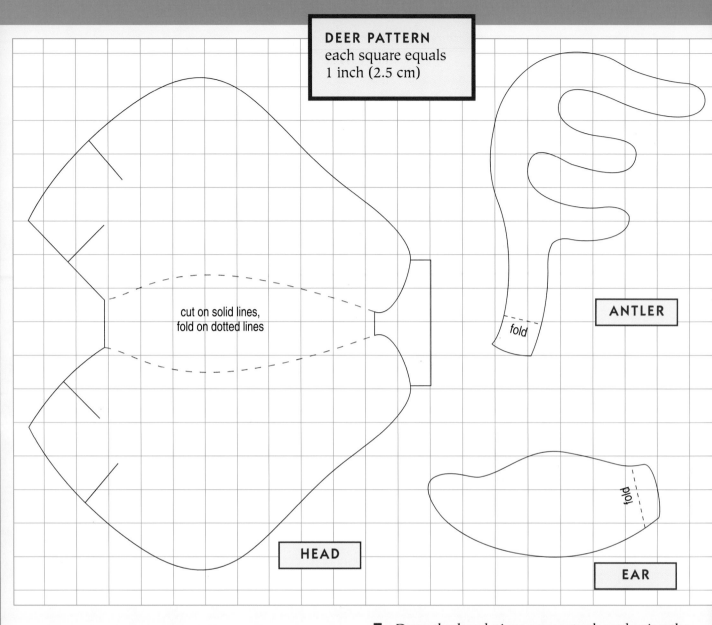

DEER PATTERN
each square equals
1 inch (2.5 cm)

cut on solid lines,
fold on dotted lines

ANTLER

fold

HEAD

fold

EAR

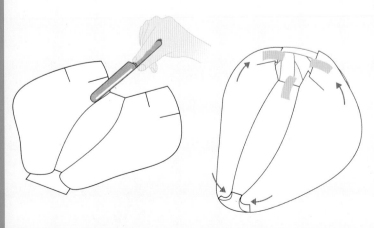

5 Draw the head piece on poster board using the pattern provided. Cut along the solid lines. Do not cut along the dotted lines indicated.

6 To make a curved crease, gently score along the fold line with a table knife. Do not cut through the poster board. Run your thumbnail along the fold line of the poster board bending the other side up against your thumb.

7 Glue the center of the forehead to the front of the paper cap, as shown. Tape in place. Gently fold the side pieces around the curve of the cap, overlapping the cut ends. Glue and tape in place.

8 Overlap the ends of the side pieces over the center piece of the nose, as shown. Glue and tape in place.

9 Using the pattern on p68, draw 2 ear shapes on poster board. Cut out. Fold 1/2 in (1 cm) from the base of the ears. Glue the folded end to the sides of the head.

10 Cut scraps of poster board and glue to the back of the cap to cover any spaces.

11 Using the pattern on p68, draw 2 antler shapes on corrugated cardboard. Cut out. Fold 1 in (2.5 cm) from the base of the antler. Glue and tape the folded end of each antler to the top of the head.

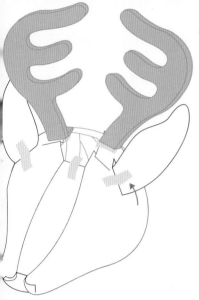

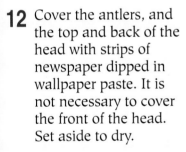

12 Cover the antlers, and the top and back of the head with strips of newspaper dipped in wallpaper paste. It is not necessary to cover the front of the head. Set aside to dry.

13 Paint.

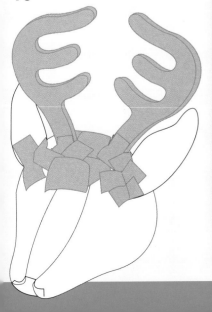

CLOWN

FACE PAINTING

TECHNIQUE Whole face painting

MATERIALS water-based face paint: white, red, blue, green, purple • brushes • make-up sponge • tissues • cotton swabs • headband

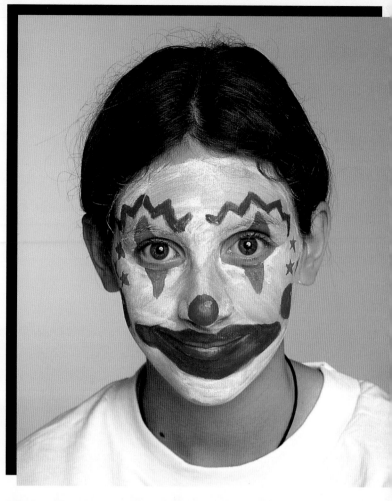

1 Using the make-up sponge, paint the entire face white.

2 Paint blue triangles above and below the eyes. Draw blue stars at the outside corners of the eyes.

3 Draw purple zig-zags along the eyebrows. Using purple, draw a large mouth shape, and fill in with purple.

4 Fill in the area between the eyebrows and eyes with green.

5 Paint a large red circle on each cheek. Paint a smaller red circle on the tip of the nose. Paint small white circles on each red circle, as shown.

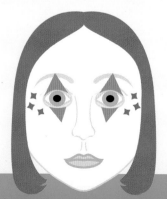

LADYBUG

FACE PAINTING

TECHNIQUE Whole face painting

MATERIALS water-based face paint: red, black • brushes • make-up sponge • tissues • cotton swabs • headband

1 Starting between the eyes, using black face paint, draw a curved line along the cheek to the outside corner of the eye. Repeat under the other eye, and connect the 2 lines by drawing an arch across the forehead, as shown.

2 Using red face paint, draw a line down the cheek from the outside corner of the black shape to the chin, and up under the lip. Repeat on the other cheek. Draw along the black lines under the eyes, as shown.

3 Fill in the red shape with solid red. Fill in the black shape with black. Leave the area around the eyes unpainted.

4 With black paint, draw antennae on the top of the head. Draw 3 legs on each cheek next to the red body. Paint black circles on top of the red body.

Protective Masks

Athletes often use masks for protection while playing their sport. A goalie in a hockey game, for example, wears a mask that is often carefully painted with the team colors and logo. Sometimes the mask is painted with a fierce animal head that might distract the opposing players. Other sports also require masks used as special equipment, such as scuba divers and fencers.

Some people require masks to do their jobs. Firefighters wear gas masks to protect them from smoke, and welders wear a mask to protect their eyes from the light of the arc welder and sparks. Police also wear masks for protection, and doctors and dentists wear masks to protect their patients from germs.

GOALIE

MASK

This mask is meant for dress-up. It is not meant to be constructed for protection.

TECHNIQUE Basic paper strip mask

MATERIALS 8-1/2 x 11 in (21.5 x 30 cm) sheets of bond paper or stiff paper • scissors • paper hole punch • craft glue • tape • 12 in (30 cm) elastic cord • paint

1 Make a basic paper strip mask, p5.

2 Paint. The mask may be painted with the logo of the team, or may be painted to resemble the team mascot or symbol (for example, a lion).

3 Attach the elastic cord, see p5.

SPACE HELMET

MASK

This mask is meant for dress-up. It is not meant to be constructed for protection.

TECHNIQUE Basic papier-mâché strip mask over a balloon

MATERIALS 12 in (30 cm) balloon • newspaper • ruler • 1 gallon (4 *l*) pail • measuring cups • box of wallpaper paste • water • string • craft knife • pen • craft glue • silver-colored duct tape • paint • green plastic pop bottle • flexible duct hose

1 To make the mask shell, follow instructions on page 8.

2 Draw the eye opening in place, see p4 (Proportions).

3 Cut off the top and bottom of a green plastic pop bottle. Cut down one side of the center to make a flat plastic sheet.

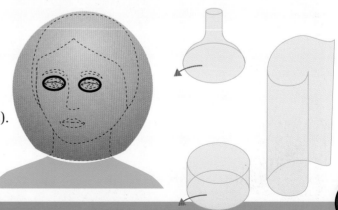

4 Place the plastic sheet over the eye markings and trace around it.

5 Draw another line 1/2 in (1 cm) inside the first line, and cut out eye opening, as shown.

6 Cover the opening with the plastic sheet. Tape in place with duct tape.

7 Place the the flexible hose on top of the shell, and draw around it. Remove the hose.

8 Cut out the inside of the circle, leaving 1/2 in (1 cm) around the inside, as shown.

9 Place the end of the hose over the opening and tape in place using duct tape.

10 Prime and paint the helmet.

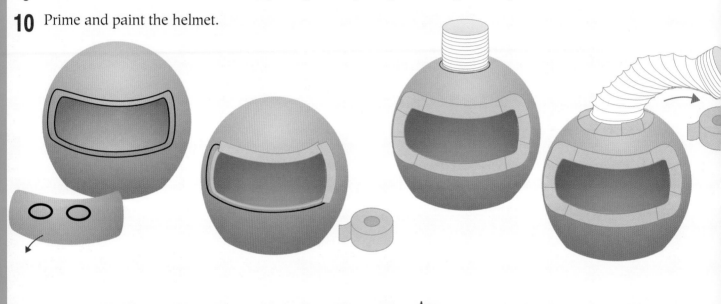

GAS MASK

MASK

TECHNIQUE   Basic papier-mâché strip mask

MATERIALS   plastic-covered styrofoam head form or plastic-covered ball of newspaper (p7) • newspaper • ruler • 1 gallon (4 *l*) pail • measuring cups • box of wallpaper paste • water • plastic wrap • plasticine • 12 in (30 cm) elastic cord • scissors • pencil • masking tape • paint • 2 plastic yogurt cups • clear plastic pop bottle • duct tape • black electrical tape

1 Make a basic papier-mâché strip mask, p8.

2 When making the plasticine form, build up the area of the nose into a cover, as shown. Model the rest of the face in a smooth shell.

3 Press 2 plastic yogurt cups into the plasticene face to resemble gas mask filters.

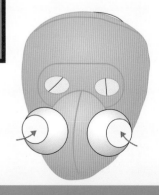

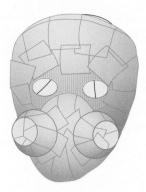

4 Cover the plasticine form and the plastic cups with strips of newspaper dipped in wallpaper paste.

5 When dry, remove the mask from the form. Trim the edges. Punch small holes in the ends of the yogurt cups so that the wearer can breathe. Make holes on either side of the mask for the elastic.

6 Cut out the eye area, as shown.

7 Prime and paint the mask.

8 Cut off the top and bottom of a clear plastic pop bottle. Cut down one side of the center to make a flat plastic sheet.

9 Trim the plastic sheet to cover the eye opening and overlap 1/2 in (1 cm).

10 Cover the opening with the plastic sheet. Tape in place with the duct tape. Cover the duct tape with black electrician's tape.

11 Attach the elastic cord, p8.

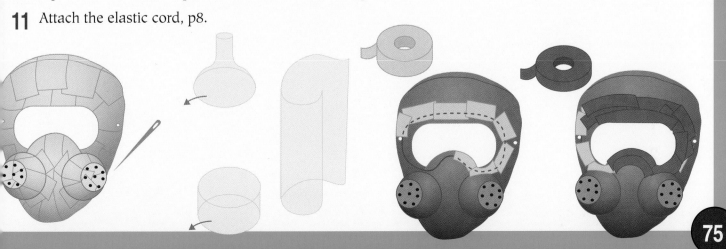

Sports

Many sports teams or organizations have a mascot. This character is designed and named, and someone wears the costume to meet the public or do publicity work. Often the mascot at a sports event will do stunts or cheer on the team and work with the crowd to make the game more fun for the spectators. The character usually has a full body costume, and a large mask or head covering that has a cartoon quality. Theme parks often have many characters portrayed by persons in costumes with complete head coverings.

TECHNIQUE Basic papier-mâché strip mask over a balloon

MATERIALS 12 in (30 cm) balloon • newspaper • ruler • 1 gallon (4 *l*) pail • measuring cups • box of wallpaper paste • water • string • craft knife • fine sandpaper • pen • craft glue • masking tape • paint • scissors • mop head replacement • warm glue gun or epoxy glue • fabric dye

MASK

Each clown's face is individual, but is usually based on a white background with multicolored designs. Many clowns have a large red mouth and exaggerated eyebrows.

1 To make the mask shell, follow instructions on page 8.

2 With a sharp knife *carefully* cut a circular opening in the open end of the shell. Continue to trim the opening until it is large enough to fit over the head. The top of the shell should rest comfortably on the top of the head of the wearer.

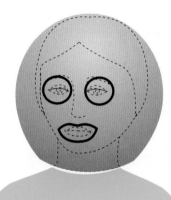

3 Fit the shell over the head to determine where the eye holes and mouth should fall. See p4 (Proportions). Mark the position of the eyes and mouth with a pen. Remove the shell from the head, then draw the eye shapes and mouth shape in place. Cut out the eyes and mouth holes.

4 Crumple a sheet of newspaper into the desired nose shape. Add more paper as required, and tape the crumpled paper in place on the front of the mask, as shown. Crumple smaller pieces of paper to form eyebrows and lips. Tape in place.

5 Mix a small quantity of wallpaper paste. Tear newspaper into small pieces. Use the paper and paste to cover the crumpled newspaper additions to the face. If a smooth edge is desired around the cut edges of the eyes and mouth, wrap paper dipped in paste around these edges. Set aside to dry.

6 When the paper is dry, sand any rough edges smooth. Paint the head, as desired. Glue the mop head replacement to the top of the mask for hair. Color or trim the hair, as desired. This hair was colored using fabric dye. Follow the package directions to dye the mop.

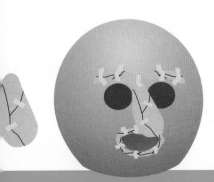

77

BEAR MASCOT

MASK

This mask presents a friendly image to a younger child. Children are usually attracted to animal imagery.

TECHNIQUE Basic papier-mâché strip mask over a balloon

MATERIALS 9 in (23 cm) balloon • newspaper • ruler • 1 gallon (4 *l*) pail • measuring cups • box of wallpaper paste • water • string • craft knife • fine sandpaper • pen • craft glue • masking tape • paint • scissors • fake fur • warm glue gun or epoxy glue • felt

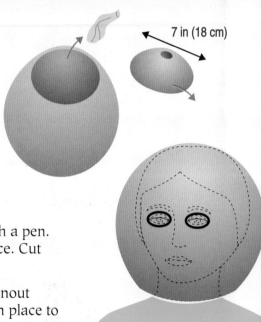

7 in (18 cm)

1 To make the mask shell, follow instructions on page 8.

2 With a sharp knife *carefully* cut a 7 in (18 cm) diameter circular opening in the open end of the shell. Remove this top in one piece to be used in step 4. Continue to trim the opening until it is large enough to fit over the head. The top of the shell should rest comfortably on top of the head of the wearer.

3 Fit the shell over the head to determine where the eye holes should be. See p4 (proportions). Mark the position of the eyes with a pen. Remove the shell from the head, then draw each eye shape in place. Cut out the eye holes.

4 From the shape cut earlier for the opening of the mask, cut out a snout approximately 4 in (20 cm) in diameter. Glue and tape this cone in place to form the bear's snout.

5 Crumple a small piece of newspaper into a ball, as shown. Tape this ball onto the center of the snout.

6 Cut out 2 ear shapes from the remaining scraps of shell, as shown.

7 Using the craft knife, *carefully* make 2 cuts in the top of the head, as shown, to hold the ears. Slide the ear pieces into the holes. Adjust the length of the cut to fit. Glue and tape in place.

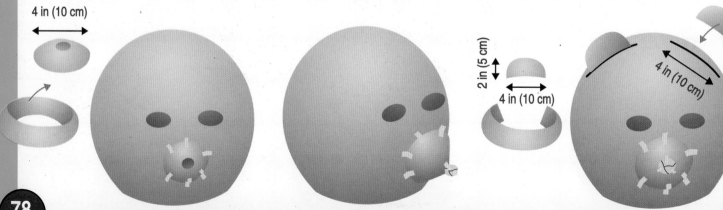

4 in (10 cm)

2 in (5 cm)

4 in (10 cm)

4 in (10 cm)

8 Cover the joins of the snout and ears with more strips of paper dipped in wallpaper paste, or pieces of paper spread with glue.

9 When dry, cover the snout and inside of the ears with felt. Cover the rest of the head with fake fur, if desired, or paint.

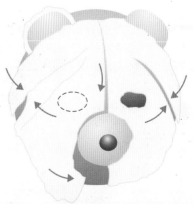

Index